GOODBYE SHIRLEY

The Wartime Letters of an Oxford Schoolboy
1939 – 1947

Michael Hickey

Edited and Narrated by

DAVID BEBBINGTON

Grosvenor House
Publishing Limited

The right of David Bebbington to be identified as the author of this
work has been asserted in accordance with Section 78
of the Copyright, Designs and Patents Act 1988

The book cover is copyright to David Bebbington

This book is published by
Grosvenor House Publishing Ltd
Link House
140 The Broadway, Tolworth, Surrey, KT6 7HT.
www.grosvenorhousepublishing.co.uk

A CIP record for this book
is available from the British Library

ISBN 978-1-78623-493-3

Contents

Foreword

by Will Wyatt

Welcome to a schoolboy's eye view of the Second World War. Shirley Hickey won a choral scholarship to become a boarder at Magdalen College School, Oxford, at the very outset of war and wrote home for the duration.

His letters form the spine of this utterly delightful and often funny book. They embrace the immediate concerns of a boy's life: requesting more lemon cheesecakes and digestive biscuits for his tuck box, asking for money 'as we have to buy a present for Pitts', apologising for, or celebrating his position in class, reporting thefts in the dorm, the spread of mumps and his excitement at learning to dance for the boat club bash.

As a chorister the young Hickey sings daily in the college chapel. The choir's work, his own performances and his musical discoveries provide a diverting ostinato to school life.

He sends his Christmas lists: a bicycle lamp, a good board game and books – 'Britain's Glorious Navy', and 'How to Draw Planes, by a man called Wootton.' Young Hickey was no mean artist, sprinkling his letters with sketches of warships in battle order, warplanes in flight, cartoons of Hitler, of the postman carrying letters and of himself exhausted by writing.

The war is a rarely far away. To fool the Germans Hickey writes from 'somewhere in England.' He boasts with patriotic schoolboy bravado, 'Have you heard that Hitler is going to raid England tomorrow? If he does, he'll have a kick in the pants he'll never forget'. Later he went to see Noel Coward's film 'In Which We Served' and 'blubbed'. Oxford was spared aerial bombardment - the only casualty was killed by a dummy RAF bomb falling by accident – but attacks were expected and the schoolboys took their turn as firewatchers.

David Bebbington uses the letters elegantly, providing a commentary on young Hickey's life and telling the larger story of the war in Oxford, illustrated with extracts and headlines from the local newspapers. I learned much that I did not know about Oxford's war and was charmed by the personal story.

Will Wyatt
October 2018

Preface

The Second World War continues to hold a fascination for many people today. Just twenty-one years after the Great War, it shaped the world more than any other event of the 20th Century. Over seven decades since its conclusion, the stories of the six-year struggle are remembered in books and films that have become part of British culture. Most of these are portrayals of war on the fighting fronts, of battles and of leaders. Stories of the struggle on the home front have become more common, but a story through a schoolboy's eyes are special. Michael Hickey was such a schoolboy who wrote home from Oxford to his parents in Stafford during the entirety of the war and for two years beyond, into peace time. These were times governed by wartime procedure and rationing. Michael's letters paint a picture of life and give a view of a city and University at the heart of the intelligence race during the war. He also recorded a chorister's view of ritual within a century-old institution during a period of turmoil.

Michael's letters take one on his journey through childhood to young manhood, during the monumental years of the 1940s. Initially preoccupied with dinky toys and fishing Michael's character matures, navigating his first kiss, starting to smoke and slowly becoming politically aware. Michael's observations of the city and the major events at the time are buttressed with local Oxford newspaper reports and headlines alluded to in his letters, capturing the atmosphere of the time to give the reader a sense of passage through the war years as seen through the eyes of an Oxford schoolboy.

Born on 16th September 1929 and baptised Shirley Michael Wright Hickey, Michael was given the first name of Shirley after his godfather, Shirley Timmis. Until the 1930s the name Shirley had been borne by men and women alike but following the fame of the child starlet Shirley Temple and her Hollywood films in the 1930s, it became a firmly feminine name. With a girl's name, Michael was vulnerable to mickey-taking and received a hard time at school. Famously, the

British wrestler Shirley Crabtree[1] (b.1928), 'Big Daddy', also had to contend with schoolboy ribbing with his schoolmates calling him Shirley Temple. Seizing the opportunity to reinvent himself on starting at Magdalen College School, Michael adopts his second name as his signature name, only reverting back to Shirley out of respect when writing to his uncle. After a term and a half at the school, and having grown in confidence and being much more sure of himself, Michael reverts back to signing his name as Shirley, respecting his parents' choice of first name for him. In 1946, with the war now over, Michael entered the last five terms of his school education and geared himself for the wider world. As if starting a fresh, like much of the country after six years war, Michael finally says goodbye to Shirley for good.

---

[1] Shirley Crabtree claimed that his father had called him Shirley because the name would be character building. His father himself was called Shirley, believed most likely due to his mother's fondness for the Charlotte Brontë novel *Shirley*. Before publication of the novel, Shirley was an uncommon but distinctly male name. Today it is regarded as a distinctly female name and an uncommon male name.

Acknowledgements

I first met Michael Hickey in 2005 when he was invited to a question-and-answer session at his old school to discuss what it had been like in Oxford and at MCS during the war. I did not meet up with him again until 2012 when, during the research and writing of my first book, 'Mister Brownrigg's Boys', I contacted Michael to see if he would be willing to have a look at my first drafts of the introductory chapters of my story of MCS and The Great War. Upon telling Michael of my project and work, he immediately showed great excitement and relief that someone was showing such interest in the school and its history. This was a huge relief to me, after being slightly wary of the 'old chorister', who had the rank of Colonel and was an honoured and recognised military historian and author. With Michael's full endorsement of the project I was able to tap into a link between the school and The Great War I didn't realise existed. Michael's grandfather (Godfrey) and great uncle (Vivian) had both been at the school in the 1880s and 1890s, and knew many of those from MCS that served during The Great War. Michael's father (Brian) had also been at the school from 1907 to 1914, and had himself served during the war and been wounded on the Somme. The Old Boy club and school network was very strong and I found that Michael had stories of many of the boys and men I was writing about, passed down to him from his grandfather and father, and from other boys previously at the school. The school that Michael inhabited in the 1940s, its routines and rituals had changed relatively little since his grandfather's day and he enthusiastically shared his memories of Oxford, 'his' school and times gone by.

On my penultimate visit to see Michael, shortly before his death in November 2013, I climbed the stairs to his bedroom, where by this time he had been restricted due to his deteriorating health. Still enthusiastic and wanting to answer my questions, it was evident that he also had something else occupying his mind. 'I want to show you something.' he said, tapping on a black box file that lay on his bed beside him. 'You must promise me that you will do something with them, publish them, then deposit them in the school archive'. With a gulp, I agreed, but I still didn't know exactly what was in the box. Upon opening the file, he revealed a muddle of letters which Michael described as 'in a bit of a mess'. This treasure trove was a collection of all, or nearly all of Michael's letters written and sent home to his parents in Stafford during his eight years of boarding at MCS. Over the subsequent years, the one hundred letters had become mixed and muddled. Only twenty-one of the letters had a full date on them, most had only the day of the week on and many had no date at all, not even a year. Before entrusting the letters to me, Michael had belatedly tried to scrawl his best guess of a date, school term or year on some of the letters. Alas, time plays cruel tricks with precision of memory and many of Michael's date guesses were a long way off and misleading. I like to think that it was Michael's way of testing my thoroughness in research, dangling a tempting and easy timestamp on some letters, that would come back to embarrass me if I didn't do a thorough job.

It had always been Michael's intention to publish the letters in some form, to tell a story of Oxford and the school during the Second World War, via the words captured in the letters written at the time. But time itself caught up with Michael. I was honoured and excited that Michael recognised in me a way of seeing his final project to fruition.

I owe Bridget, Michael's widow, a big debt of gratitude for her continual interest and encouragement of the project and for our periodic coffee and biscuit meetings at every school holiday. Bridget has supplied me with snippets of information and photos that have helped to piece together Michael's family structure and friends mentioned in the letters and to chronicle his post-school life for the postscript. For this, together with her friendship, fresh coffee and shortbreads I am eternally grateful.

I would like to thank Oxfordshire County Council - Oxfordshire History Centre for the kind permission to reproduce images from their microfiche collection of the *Oxford Mail* and *The Oxford Times* and of the Centaur Tank at Morris Motors, Magdalen College School for access to their archive and permission to reproduce images of the 'Saga on the Cherwell', and Bridget for permission to reproduce images from Michael's personal photographic collection. If in the few cases where, despite every effort, the copyright owners for images were not traceable, if they come to light in the future the relevant acknowledgement will be published in subsequent editions of this book.

Three proof readers extraordinaire, Deb my wife, Alan Cooper (teacher and MCS oracle) and Peter McDonald (teacher and grammarian), devoted much time making corrections and suggestions. I am eternally grateful to them for knocking the book into shape and for their wonderful encouragement and advice.

I am very grateful to Deb, and my children Aggie and Sam for accepting and understanding my regular announcement to the household that 'I'm going to do some work on the book' and for putting up with me constantly talking about Michael, MCS, Oxford and the Second World War. Without their support and encouragement, I would not have been able to complete the project. Thank you.

Chapter 1

..... on the eve of war

Oxford ....

By the late 1930s Oxford was becoming an important and prosperous city not only because of its thriving and continually expanding University but also because of its burgeoning manufacturing industry, with the likes of the Pressed Steel Company, Osberton Radiator Company and Morris Motors. The city boundaries were increased in 1929 and the population of the extended city area grew by twenty percent between 1921 and 1931, mainly via migration from economically distressed areas of the country, particularly the south-west and South Wales. During this time, Oxford's population growth was only exceeded by two other towns in the country, so by 1936, Oxford was ranked jointly as the most prosperous town in the country along with Coventry and Luton. To cope with the increased population, approximately 2,000 new corporation homes were built in the decade leading up to the start of the war, including estates at Rose Hill, Freelands, Gipsy Lane, Cutteslowe, South Park and Weir's Lane. Private developers also built approximately 5,000 new homes, mainly in North Oxford and the areas previously around and outside the city boundary. Large numbers of North Oxford's enormous houses were also converted into flats. The recently built Police Station (1936), the rebuilding of the New Theatre (1933), the opening of a new park at Hinksey (1934), significant funding of the orthopaedic centre (to become the Nuffield Orthopaedic Centre after the local benefactor, William Morris, Viscount Nuffield), the building of the New Bodleian Library (1937-40) and the opening of Oxford Airport (1938) all gave the feel of a thriving and vibrant area.

In the Autumn of 1939 with the threat of bombing to London and other major cities, the population of Oxford was further swollen with an influx of people, including official evacuees from major cities who were billeted in Oxford homes, and unofficial evacuees who retreated to the relatively safe haven of Oxford by staying with relatives. Many of the capital's Government departments and military services also relocated into college buildings and accommodation.

London University medical students took over Keble, Wadham and St Peter's Hall. Balliol became host to the Royal Institute of International Affairs and St John's to the Director of Fish Supplies, causing Oxford to be humorously referred to as the centre of the fishing industry, despite being almost as far from the sea that you can get in Britain. The Ministry of Transport took over most of Merton and the Ministry of Home Security was housed by Queen's. Brasenose accommodated several military schools and Oriel housed the War Office intelligence corps. The previously largely male-dominated academic environments of the Oxford colleges (apart from the then women's colleges of Lady Margaret Hall, Somerville, St Hugh's and St Hilda's) were suddenly transformed by an invasion of female clerks associated with these departments and services and the influx of female staff from London hospitals.

In September 1939 Oxford was settling down to war conditions and restrictions and on the morning of Wednesday 6th September, the city heard its first air raid warning and the official announcement of fuel control for petrol and coal, to start on 1st October, was published by *The Oxford Times*.

The School ….

Throughout the 1930s, numbers attending Magdalen College School had been approximately 150-160, but by as early in the war as 1939 this number jumped to 192. The impression that Oxford was a 'safe city', immune to German bombing, is thought to have contributed to the trend of boys being evacuated from threatened towns and cities to Oxford and its schools, with many ending up boarding at MCS. Several boys taken in as boarders by the school were refugees from Eastern Europe. Sadly, recollections of these times by two old boys of the school indicate these refugees were regrettably subjected to anti-Semitic bullying by some boarders. As evacuees and refugees continued to migrate to Oxford during the war, requests to accommodate more boys were continuously received and the school's roll increased significantly to 207 in 1941, 229 in 1942 and 291 in 1944. The increased numbers were accommodated by the school by gradually duplicating its forms throughout the school until by 1949 it was educating 400 boys.

Traditionally a fee-paying school, of the 192 boys on the school roll in September 1939, fifty-nine of the boys were either not charged a fee, or were on scholarships, or the fees were paid by the City Council. The school accommodated approximately sixty boarders within its 'School House', with the remainder being day-boys living at home within the local area. Michael, from Stafford, boarded at the school for all eight years of his attendance.

The School was considerably smaller and a very poor relation to other Public or private schools in terms of facilities, buildings and endowments, with 'School House' only having a solitary indoor toilet for the boys and the outdoor latrine facilities, known as the 'Woods', being at best primitive. MCS had more the feel of, and could be considered more similar to, a 1940s Grammar School. Caps, ties and blazers were worn and boys called each other by their surname or nickname. The two Master's (as the headmaster is known) during the war, Kennard Davis (until 1944) and Bob Stanier (from 1944), gave the boys a liberal and fairly cultured education. In 1939 the school had nine full-time and two part-time teaching masters but was preparing to replace staff under the age of thirty who were liable for 'call-up' to the war, and to add extra staff members if possible in order to cope with a predicted increase in pupils. Soon after the start of the war, the school temporarily replaced the three teachers who had been called up for active service (the boarding housemaster 'Flick' Simmonds, who re-joined the army; Ronald Reynolds, a physics teacher, and Edgar L. Russell, a maths teacher, who both joined the Navy) with a remarkable collection of retired teachers. Additionally, and unusually for the school at the time, a female teacher, Miss Jarvis, known as 'Ma Ja', was also taken on in 1941 to help teach the increasing numbers attending the school during the war.[2] All three teachers who left for active service returned safely to MCS to continue their teaching after the war.

Within School House there were three boarding dormitories, 'Senior', 'Junior' and 'Baby' dorm, with twenty-four iron bedsteads in each of the first two and twelve in the Baby dorm, each with their own chamber pot. Only one 'Victorian' loo (principally the housemaster's toilet) was available at night, but due to this being on the first floor, below the Junior and Baby dorms, it was considered too hazardous a journey for boys from those two dorms to attempt at night. Down the centre of each dorm were wash stands, each holding four basins, china jugs, towels and soap. In a separate wing of the building was the Master's accommodation. The school Matron also lived in School House and looked after the general health of the boys, administering medicines as needed. Boils were subjected to boiling hot poultices, and then if not complying they were lanced! Anyone with sore throats had their tonsils 'painted' and had to gargle with a solution described by Michael to be 'like horse's urine'. Cod liver oil, malt (Radio Malt™) and Ministry of Food orange juice were given routinely to help the

---

[2] Miss Ismay Jarvis (later Mrs Holloway) was thought at the time to have been the first female to teach at MCS. However the staff roll in Examination Lists of 1900 and *The Lily* magazine of November 1899 record a Miss Baker joining MCS to teach the youngest form.

boys stay healthy and to 'bulk them up'. For pimples and small boils, garlic pills were taken. If a boy had a minor malaise, he would be sent for bed rest in his dorm. If he had more alarming symptoms he would be confined to the sick room to be watched by the beady eye of Matron. The Hilary term (January – April) usually featured some sort of epidemic, eg. measles, mumps, chicken pox or gastric flu. In addition, aided by the senior house domestics 'Ann' and 'Phipps', Matron did the boarders' washing and mended their clothes. Changes of clothes however were infrequent and Michael recalled only having two changes of underwear and socks per week. Other members of the domestic staff, presided over by the Master's wife, were the Cook and her assistant 'Greasy Joan', who reigned over the scullery, and a succession of caretaker figures who provided a shoe-cleaning service for the boarders and stoked the unreliable boiler that fed the central heating system.

In 1939 Milham Ford Girls' School, at the time located next to MCS on Cowley Place, moved to new premises in Marston. Later that year the vacated cottage building and several wooden huts used as classrooms were briefly occupied by St Clement Danes Boys School (SCDS), after being evacuated from Hammersmith, London. The SCDS boys were subsequently found school places at Southfield Grammar (Cowley), New College and local village hall schools, allowing MCS to take over and use the wooden huts on Milham Ford Field as extra classrooms for the expanding school. This was just as well, because although the boys from SCDS and MCS didn't have a lot of contact with each other, a certain amount of edginess and antipathy grew between the two sets of boys in the few months they were neighbours.

The typical school day for a boarder at MCS started at 07:30, when a hand bell was rung around the dorms by one of the domestics. The boys filled jugs for the bathrooms, washed, cleaned their teeth and dressed. At 08:00 a roll call was answered with the word 'sum' (Latin for I am present) by each boy, then at 08:15 a breakfast of cereal or porridge, bacon, tinned tomatoes, 'scrambled eggs' made with powder ('foul stuff' Michael grimaced), and sometimes potato, bread and margarine, was taken. This could be augmented with food from home, eg. butter, jams, marmalade, eggs and baked beans. Breakfast was washed down with tea from jugs. In the summer, compulsory Physical Training (PT) was performed on the field before breakfast.

Nearly all day-boys who lived within the Oxford city boundary came to school by bicycle, parking them in the long bicycle shed beside the playground. David Mander, a day-boy at MCS from 1942-49, admitted that 'Cycling did have some attraction, for you might catch the eye of one of the girls also riding to school – at Milham Ford, St Faith's or the High School.' Day-boys from the country would arrive by bus at Gloucester Green bus station, then walk the mile or so through the town and colleges.

At 09:00 there would either be school chapel for a ten minute 'act of worship', or 'Big School' once a week when any special announcements were made, followed by a further 15 minutes of Physical Training. Then followed four periods of lessons each morning, although at this point in the day Michael and the other choristers were taken out of class and marched 'crocodile order' over to Magdalen College for choir practice (in gowns, mortarboards and Eton collars), missing lessons considered of little importance such as drawing or singing (under Mr Burton). The sixteen choristers practised each morning for the seven Evensongs sung every week of the University term.

At mid-morning break, playground hockey was popular which saw a free-for-all with primitive sticks, not unlike inverted walking sticks. Milk (⅓ pint) was provided in bottles for the younger boys, while older boys were allowed to visit local 'tuck' shops. Popular were, the sweet and tobacconist shop on the opposite side of the Plain owned by Mr and Mrs Blackwell where boys would regularly purchase penny buns; and 'Daddy Dance', a shop on the Cowley Road that had been run by old Mr Dance since Michael's father's time at the school, where 'for a penny, one could indulge in a luridly coloured fizzy drink called 'Vantas' and a bag of broken crisps'.

At 12:30 a boarders' lunch was served in School House at two long tables for the boys, sitting in a rough order of seniority, plus a High

Table for the masters and prefects. The lunch usually consisted of meat, curry, mince or fish (described by Michael as 'dried cod boiled in decorator's paste'), followed by a pudding (either suet, trifle, dried fruit and custard, semolina and jam - 'Tragedy in the Alps', rice or sago pudding). Michael recollected the school food as meagre and dreadful, and many boys used to escape after meal times, climbing a high wall by the outside lavatories, to supplement their diet with chips, or fish if affluent, from the nearby local chip shop in St Clement's Street, remembering 'a bag of chips .... cost two pence and an alarmingly pink battered sausage a similar amount'. Things did however significantly improve when Bob Stanier became headmaster in 1944, his wife Maida Stanier, taking it upon herself to improve the school's food provision. For day-boys, lunch was obtained by a brief return home or from the 'Munie' or British Restaurant, a Municipal Restaurant on York Place in St Clement's,[3] although for some older boys a quick trip down to the snooker hall in the centre of town seems to have been an alternative lunch time attraction! At 14:00, except for Wednesday, it was back to lessons followed by Games in the late afternoon. On Wednesdays Officers' Training Corps or Scouts[4] (and later Cubs) was attended in uniform. Some Friday afternoons, OTC was attended in mufti.[5] School ended at 16:00 for day-boys, but for the boarders it was first tea then free time. For Michael and the other choristers however,

---

[3] Basic two course meals were served on battered pressed metal trays for about 1s 3d, later rising to about 1s 8d, equivalent to just less than £2 today. 'The potatoes were lumpy and grey, the lump of bread was 'utility' standard and if you got damsons and custard, that day was a treat.' Michael however recalled that the boarders would envy the dayboys' ability to go to these National Restaurants where a seemingly more wholesome lunch than in School House was obtained at a reasonable price, one shilling for a main course of stew and vegetables. As well as the 'Munie' in St Clement's, the City council ran Municipal or 'British' restaurants in Headington, Gloucester Green and at the Town Hall.

[4] The 40th Oxford Scout Group. The troop flag at the time, made by Ma D, was black with the school's white lily embroidered on it. Brian Bennett (Troop Leader) remembered carrying it at the St George's Day procession along the High Street to the service in the cathedral.

[5] Mufti refers to plain or ordinary clothes, especially when worn by someone who normally wears a uniform. Another common similar meaning slang is civvies, which refers to civilian attire.

there was the routine of Evensong in the College Chapel at 18:15 (in 1941, the evensong service time changed to 17:30).[6] Between 18:30 – 19:30 prep was done in the Dining Hall, followed by cocoa and 'Dorm' for IVth Form and below. Prayers then lights out was at 21:00, though a 'Dorm book' was permitted. This was also the time during which punishments or 'binchings' were administered by prefects, with boys receiving any caning they were due in pyjama bottoms so that little protection would soften the blows. Michael received his fair share of the cane, and recalled receiving several whacks for relatively minor infringements, like straying too close to or playing in the river. Finally, seniors went to their Dorms by 22:00.

On Saturdays there were lessons in the morning, then Games in the afternoon.[7]

After school on Saturday and all day on Sunday the boarders were free to explore Oxford and many took the opportunity to visit the city's museums and colleges. In the absence of a decent school library they also used to frequent the City library in St Aldate's.

---

[6] Much of their free time was spent by boys in their allocated, mixed age studies. The five studies were aptly named to identify their location in the School House, Bottom end, Middle end, Middle middle, Top end and Top middle. Furniture for the study was either inherited from previous occupants or brought in from home.

[7] The school games during this era were: Autumn: Rugby; Spring: Hockey and Rowing; Summer: Cricket, Tennis, Rowing and Athletics.

Michael .....

On Friday 5th May 1939 Shirley Michael Wright Hickey travelled by steam train, from his home in Stafford, to Oxford to undergo an audition for the prestigious Magdalen Choir and hopefully with it, a place at Magdalen College School (MCS, founded 1480). Up to the age of ten, Michael had attended St Leonard's Primary School in Stafford, a short walk from where he lived at 45 Rising Brook. Michael revelled in the fact that he 'enjoyed St Leonard's from the moment I started there', and he soon realised that his parents' encouragement of him to read widely and to attend the nearby parish church of St Paul's, to supplement his learning with a religious and musical education, was all in preparation for what he called 'the supreme test'. Michael's father, grandfather and great uncle had all been fortunate enough to be educated at MCS, but for Michael it would only be possible to take up such an educational opportunity if the financial support of a choral scholarship was achieved.[8] Of the 'small crowd of nervous boys and their apprehensive parents' attending the audition and interview that day, three boys were admitted as Choral Scholars, David Metcalfe, Barry Lyndon and Michael. The three were to remain lifelong friends. Before returning triumphant to Stafford, Michael was taken to see the school doctor, Dr Mallam, at 3 Holywell Street for a 'perfunctory check to see if I could breathe'. The same examination, by the same doctor had been performed on Michael's father, Brian, thirty-two years earlier. Despite the financial support that the scholarship gave to Michael's education, the school uniform and kit, especially for a chorister, 'imposed a heavy financial load on [his] parents', who were helped considerably by Michael's godfather, Shirley Timmis.

On the eve of his progression from local primary school boy to distant boarding chorister, Michael became conscious that 'my parents'

---

[8] Prior to 1987, Magdalen College fully funded the education of its sixteen choristers at the School.

decision to give me a Christian name that honoured my generous godfather Shirley Timmis had been a mistake; for what until the 1930s had been a name borne alike by men and women was now, following the fame of the child starlet Shirley Temple and her Hollywood films, firmly a feminine one. From this point I was in open rebellion against the use of my Christian name but it was not for many years that I was able to use my second name instead.'

Michael and his mother just prior to joining MCS in 1939

Maps

Map1. Area immediately around Magdalen College School,
The Plain, Oxford, 1939-1947.

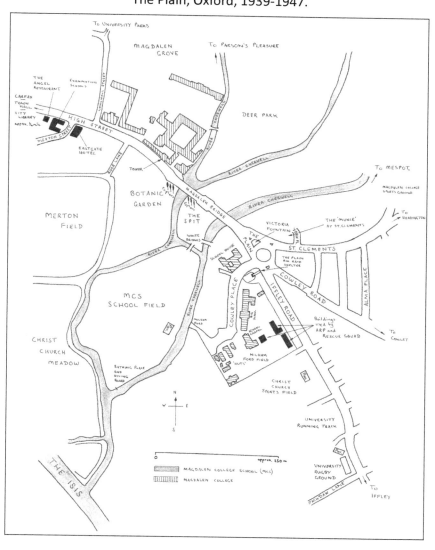

Map 2. Map of Oxford and surrounding area, 1939-1947.

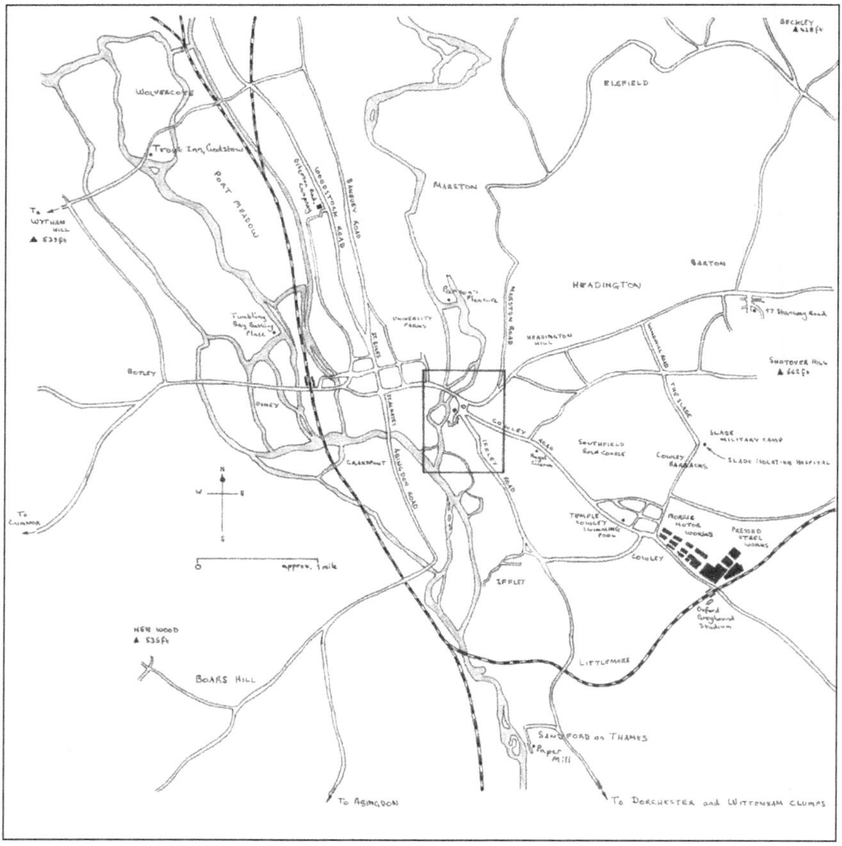

Chapter 2

Letters home

The same punctuation, spelling, letter case, bold and underlining has been used in the type-written letters as were in Michael's original hand-written letters.

Any corrections to spelling or clarification to meaning has been included in the text of the letters within square brackets [ ].

The date or part date for a letter given in square brackets [ ] indicates this is a calculated date, due to either no date at all or only the weekday being given on the original letter. If no precise date could be discerned from the information available within the letter a general date is given to guide, but not mislead the reader.

Autumn 1939 – Summer 1940

Stamp Hinges and Invasion excitement

Autumn (Michaelmas) Term 1939

Michael arrived at Magdalen College School, Oxford on Friday 22nd September 1939, less than three weeks after the declaration of war with Germany. He recalled his journey to Oxford, *'a subdued family group boarded the train at Stafford, changed trains at Wolverhampton from LMS to Great Western[9] and as mother sobbed convulsively – her preciously guarded only offspring was leaving home – I was deposited at the boarders' house at the end of Magdalen Bridge.'* Considerable precautions had already been taken in School House (where the boarders lived), blackout curtains had been fitted and the basement had been shored up with timbers and provided with anti-gas screens. The windows of Magdalen College Chapel, where as a chorister Michael was to spend a large proportion of his time, had also been blacked out. The entire population had been issued with gas masks earlier in the year and these had to be carried at all times. Food rationing would not be imposed for several months and for the time being the School House *'food was adequate but deteriorated alarmingly as the war progressed'*. All the boarders lost weight during term time and Michael recalled his weight falling *'alarmingly by up to half a stone'* each term but took great delight in remembering how he *'was fed like a prize-fighter when at home for the holidays'*. Boarders were actively encouraged to write home each week, with Sunday evenings being the prescribed time dedicated to this.

Sunday 24th September 1939

Dear Mummy and Daddy,

I'm having a simply gorgeous time here, and I have been in good health so far.

---

[9] LMS was the London, Midland and Scottish Railway Company, and Great Western was Great Western Railway (GWR) Company, two of the 'Big Four' railway companies before nationalisation in 1948.

Excuse me writing in pencil, but there is no ink in the study.[10]

There was no rugger for me yesterday.

Your loving son, Michael

Sunday 24th September was not so gorgeous a day for a home 2 ½ miles to the east of Oxford, 97 Stanway Road, Headington. At 8pm that evening a dud bomb fell from a British plane while it passed over east Oxford. The bomb fatally injured a young London evacuee. The victim, six-year-old Trevor Thomas, was asleep in bed with his brother, David, at the home of Mr and Mrs F.W. Love. The bomb smashed its way through the roof, passed through the bed on which the two boys were sleeping and embedded itself in the foundations of the house. This was to be the only fatality from an aerial bomb in Oxford during the War.

R.A.F. DUMMY BOMB WRECKS PART OF HOUSE

CHILD EVACUEE KILLED

A DUMMY bomb accidentally dropped by an R.A.F. machine exercising early yesterday wrecked the interior of 97, Stanway-road, Oxford, home of Mr. and Mrs. F. W. Love, and injured a young London evacuee. The boy, the "Oxford Mail" understands, died this morning.

The victim, Trevor Thomas, aged 6, who had come from Poplar, London, was sleeping with his brother, David.

The bomb smashed its way through the roof, passed through the bed on which the boys were sleeping, and embedded itself several feet deep in the concrete foundations of the house. All the furniture in the living room was destroyed.

RAF Dummy Bomb Wrecks Part of House. Child Evacuee Killed. *Oxford Mail*, 28th September 1939

---

[10] Michael's first year study was 'a sparsely furnished den, shared with seven or eight other junior boys'.

Tuesday 10th October 1939

Dear Mummy and Daddy,

I am very glad to know you are still alive and kicking. Our 2nd XV beat Henley grammar school 2nd XV 42-0 today.[11]

Mr Mackie [Mckie] took me up the tower[12] last Sunday, and the view is simply glorious.

There have been many study thefts recently, and, in Top Little, 2 tuckboxes have been forced!

Please excuse the terrible blot which will need good attention.[13]

Your loving son, Michael

P.S. When is Daddy's birthday?[14]

A SIGN OF THE TIMES: Magdalen Bridge almost deserted at midday – usually a peak hour for traffic.
Oxford Mail, 6th October 1939

---

[11] This game was played on Saturday 7th October 1939 and according to official records ended 41-0 to MCS 2nd XV.

[12] The tower being Magdalen College Tower, the lofty heights from which the Magdalen choristers sing every May Morning.

[13] Michael's ink pen accidently left a large blue blot on his letter.

[14] Michael's father's birthday was 18th October.

The panoramic view from the top of Magdalen Tower has changed little over hundreds of years, but the detail within the surrounding streets changed quickly and significantly in the latter months of 1939 and the beginning of 1940. Ground level air-raid shelters were built to supplement underground or basement shelters, like the one constructed at the ARP Centre on Iffley Road, opposite the MCS School House on The Plain (see below). And, water tanks were constructed at strategic places, for emergency use by fire services, similar to the one shown below outside The Queen's College.

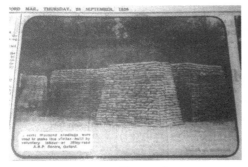

Air-raid shelter at Iffley Road ARP Centre
Oxford Mail, 28th September 1939

Construction of Water tanks
outside Queen's College
Oxford Mail, 16th December 1939

The main headline in the *Oxford Mail* of Saturday 14th October 1939, 'British Battleship Sunk', reported the demoralising loss of the battleship Royal Oak together with over one thousand crew.

BRITISH BATTLESHIP SUNK
Oxford Mail, 14th October 1939

Four days later the *Oxford Mail* reported that a great German attack across the whole of the Western front was expected.

GERMAN OFFENSIVE ON WEST EXPECTED WITHIN 24 HOURS
Oxford Mail, 18th October 1939

Settling in to his new boarding school environment occupied most of Michael's attention in the first few weeks of the Autumn term and, despite the gloomy reports about the war in the newspapers and on the wireless, he hadn't yet mentioned the conflict in his letters home. Michael, only ten years old at this time, did however indicate his awareness of the spreading conflict in Europe and the expected invasion of France, when he attempted to let Hitler know exactly what he thought of him, by including a sketch and message at the end of his next letter for his parents to send to the German leader.

[mid-October 1939]

Dear Mummy and Daddy,

I am looking very forward to Sunday, but I'm afraid you'll miss matins, which starts at 9.30am.

The Lyndon boys can come also.

Also I wish Daddy many happy returns; please accept my little gift, as it took 5d out of existence.

Here is a list of the things I need.

Penknife, 2 pkts digestive biscuits, and many more other small thing <u>you</u> think would be useful to me.

Your loving son, Michael.

Michael's picture drawn at the end of his [mid-October 1939] letter. With the instruction 'post this to Hitler, it's called 'the Kultured pig'.'

All of Michael's letters to his parents in 1939 were signed 'Michael', his second name. The letter sent to his Uncle Shirley and Aunty Brenda, below, is signed 'Shirley', his first name. It is likely that this was done so as not to offend his godfather, after whom he was named and who was contributing to the fees and costs of Michael's schooling at MCS.

[October or November] 1939

Dear Uncle Shirley and Aunty Brenda,

I am very, very thankful to you for everything that you have done. Am enjoying myself very much here; many of the chaps are pretty decent.

I send my apologies for not writing earlier in the term and my bad writing.

How is Beaconsfield getting on? I have heard about your 10 evacuees and the teacher. I may be able to write to you both next week, and definitely before the end of term. I'm afraid I'll have to close up now, and here is my very best wishes for you both.

Your thankful godson, Shirley

Despite Britain being at war with Germany since the start of September 1939, triggered by Germany's invasion of Poland, public opinion and debate about appeasement and anti-appeasement was still very heated. On Armistice Day 1939, the Oxford community awoke to find their War Memorial daubed with graffiti advocating no fighting.

Oxford War Memorial Vandalism. *Oxford Mail*,
Saturday 11th November 1939.

The realism of war came to the streets of Oxford later that week, on Thursday 16th November 1939, when a mock aerial attack on Oxford was simulated in order to 'test the [local] hospital and kindred services'. Oxford schoolboys, playing the part of the injured, were treated by steel-helmeted ambulance men who examined the labels they carried and treated them accordingly.

'400 Bomb Casualties at Oxford.'
Big test at Hospital and First Aid Services.
Oxford Mail, Friday 17th November 1939

[October or November] 1939

Dear Mother and Father,

I would like to know if rations[15] have started, and, if they haven't please send me some 'maids-of-Honour'. Also I am wondering when you are sending me that tinned food.

This afternoon I am hoping to go for a walk. The Lyndons have gone out, so that I may go by myself.

---

[15] Although petrol was immediately rationed at the start of the Second World War, food rationing, starting with bacon, butter and sugar, did not begin until 8th January 1940. This was followed by successive rationing schemes for more and more food stuffs until August 1942, when eventually all foods were rationed apart from vegetables and bread. Bread was not rationed until after the war, in July 1946.

My expeditions so far have been to 'Messpot'[16] and the main river, where I'm delighted in the 8's.

This afternoon I shall explore the Iffley Road.

Your loving son, Michael.

P.S. Thank you for your Xmas preparations

Michael's exploration of the Iffley Road led him to discover the Oxford University Rugby ground, a venue he would return to many times during his school days, to watch some prestigious games. The first wartime match that Michael attended at the Iffley Road ground was on 18th November 1939, a rainy Saturday afternoon, when a crowd of about 4,000 witnessed a Russian Prince[17] score a try to help Major Stanley's XV beat Oxford University XV by 8 points to 3 points.

An incident in the match between Major Stanley's XV (in white) and Oxford University at Oxford on Saturday. The Dark Blues were beaten 8pts to three.
Oxford Mail, Monday 20th November 1939

---

[16] 'Messpot', or more correctly 'Mespot', is short for Mesopotamia, a narrow island that is part of the University Parks, Oxford. It lies between the upper and the lower reaches of the River Cherwell.

[17] Prince Alexander Obolensky (Brasenose College, 1934, England, 1936), 'The Flying Prince', was killed the following year, age 24, during RAF training when his Hawker Hurricane plane crashed on Martlesham Heath, Suffolk. See *Oxford Mail*, Saturday 30th March 1940, Death of Prince Obolensky – An Oxford Hero, for a full report.

[Sunday 19th November] 1939

Dear Mother and Father,

Thank you both very much for the 3 parcels which you sent me. Matron won't let me have the third parcel, and she says you must not send so much grub.

Yesterday I went to see the Varsity play Major Stanley's XV at rugger. Obolensky, the international, was playing. I do hope that you don't mind an extra 1/- on the bill. I hope that no air raid warnings have been heard in Stafford. The other night, as we were coming over the bridge I saw some search light practice which looked very grand. I'm afraid I'll have to close now as I have some Latin prep.

Your loving son, Michael.

P.S. If 'Pitts'[18] does not give me that parcel the cakes might go stale and then what??!

[late November / early December] 1939

Dear Mother and Father,

I do hope you are enjoying yourselves at Trowell.[19] I received your letter with address on, so this note ought to reach you.

Please thank granny for the sausages, which were very delightful to the taste.

I will write her a postcard soon; please send my apologies to her for not writing to her separately.

When you get back tell Geoffrey to get the new Dinky Toy catalogue, unfortunately it costs 1d this year owing to the war.

---

[18] 'Pitts' was the boys' nickname for the then Matron, Elizabeth Halsey.
[19] Michael's grandfather, Rev. Godfrey M. V. Hickey, was the Rector of St Helen's Church, Trowell, Nottinghamshire.

If you buy me some tin soldiers please insist in buying khaki ones. Next week I'll tell you in full what I want for Xmas. Also, I send my very best wishes to 'Goggy' and Aunty Vera and Granny and last but not least Gangipop and you.

Your loving son, Michael

The school actively encouraged its boys to keep up to date with the progress and politics of the war by reading the local and national newspapers. These were available each day in the school library, which had been relocated to the basement of School House after the declaration of war. The cellar had its ceiling reinforced with wooden beams and was able to be made air-tight in the event of a gas attack. It is here that Michael read about the opening salvoes of Britain's war with Germany, initially mainly at sea. Fully informed and aware of the sea battle that took place on 13th December 1939, which involved the heavy cruiser HMS Exeter and the light cruisers HMS Ajax and HMS Achilles, Michael included sketches of a heavy and a light cruiser in his next letter home.

NAZI CRUISER SUNK. Torpedoed By British Submarine At Naval Base. *Oxford Mail*, Monday 18th December 1939

EPIC STORY OF EXETER. Fought Until Only One Gun Could Fire. *Oxford Mail*, Tuesday 19th December 1939

the *Oxford Mail* of Tuesday 19th December reported that the Exeter, Ajax and Achilles had all taken part in the battle with the German pocket battleship, Admiral Graf Spee. Later known as the 'Battle of the River Plate', this was the first major naval battle of the World War Two.

[mid-December] 1939

Dear Mother and Father,

I am sorry that I have written in pencil this week, but there is no ink in my pens.

Here is my list for Xmas:- A good set of tin soldiers (in khaki); a good selection of Dinky Toy men, making sure some wear tin helmets; a good science book about aeroplanes; and, if possible, a very small toy searchlight.

If anything else is wanted I will tell you.

This Xmas the choristers will have a tea-party and also we have been given money to buy presents. With my 5/- I bought a camera, which, no doubt will be used by us all. Remember that its only 10 days before I come home.

If Uncle Shirley asks me what I want this term I am thinking of a small gramophone for the study is in urgent need of one as well as Jam. I do hope you enjoyed yourselves at Trowell.

This week I'm sending one or two sketches, which perhaps you could show to Geoffrey.

Your loving son, Michael

Michael's pictures drawn at the end of his [mid-December] 1939 letter. A 'HEAVY' CRUISER (top) and A 'LIGHT' CRUISER (bottom).

At the close of the year, 1939, the Oxford public were treated to the unveiling of the new Bodleian Library extension on Broad Street. The official opening of the New Bodleian Library by the King, initially planned for Friday 21st June 1940, had to wait until after the war was over. On Wednesday 19th June 1940, it was reported in the *Oxford Mail* that Bodley's Librarian at the time, Dr H.H.E. Craster, announced 'His Majesty had consented to postpone the opening' ... until, optimistically 'the year which follows our final victory.' The King kept his promise and visited Oxford on 24th October 1946 to officially open the new library, see letter of 26th October 1946.

BODLEIAN EXTENSION REVEALED.
Oxford Mail, Wednesday 20th December 1939.

Spring (Hilary) Term 1940

As Michael's second term in Oxford dawned, the *Oxford Mail* wished its readers a 'Happy New Year'. It was quite at liberty to do so, as all was quiet in the war, so much so that the period the country was now at the mid-point of became known as the 'Phoney War'. An eight-month-stretch during which only one limited military land operation on the Western Front took place, when French troops briefly invaded Germany's Saar district. A photo and report of a collision between a skidding car and a cyclist on the Iffley Road, near the A.R.P. centre, therefore still achieved front page prominence in the *Oxford Mail* at the start of the year. Three people were injured.

HAPPY NEW YEAR. TO ALL OUR READERS.
Oxford Mail, Monday 1st January 1940

The relative 'peace' and indifference, if you ignore the several significant actions at sea, was to be shattered when Germany attacked France and the Low Countries on 10th May, eventually triggering a British retreat through France that would end in heroic rear guard actions allowing salvage of the remnants of the British Army from the channel ports, most famously Dunkirk.

[January] 1940

Dear Mother and Father,

I am very sorry to hear that 'Dad' is suffering from a cough.

Have you purchased a torch yet? If so, please send with great haste, and, if you can manage 6d in money.

I received the braces yesterday at teatime, and was attracted by their brilliance.

Talking about stamps could you send me a 'Syria' pkt from 'Smiths'.

Pitts says that you have not packed my gym shoes; if this is true please send them immediately, together with a hockey stick.

Well, goodbye till next Sunday when, if poss. I'll send the films.

Your loving son, Michael

Three headline-making visitors came to Oxford during the second half of January 1940. On 17th, the King gave a surprise visit; on 27th it was revealed that a close friend of Hitler, Unity Mitford, was convalescing in the Radcliffe Infirmary with two bullet holes in her head; and during this time the city had been visited by frosts and the coldest temperatures for forty-five years.

KING'S SURPRISE VISIT TO OXON. The report goes on to say 'Although the Royal visit had been kept as secret as possible the inhabitants of a market town 'somewhere in Oxfordshire' guessed that something unusual was afoot because of the early movements of the troops this morning. *Oxford Mail*, Wednesday 17th January 1940

Unity Mitford was the sister-in-law of Oswald Moseley, the leader of the British Union of Fascists. More crucially she was a close friend and devotee of Hitler. In January 1940, she returned to England from Germany, via Switzerland, to convalesce after attempting suicide on the outbreak of war. Under the care of neurosurgeon Professor Hugh Cairns,[20] Unity was nursed back to health in the Nuffield No.1 Ward of the Radcliffe Infirmary, then lived out her days until her death in 1948 at Swinbrook, near Burford.

UNITY MITFORD IN RADCLIFFE INFIRMARY. TWO BULLET WOUNDS IN THE HEAD. The *'Oxford Mail'* is able to reveal that Miss Unity Mitford, oldest daughter of Lord Redesdale, and friend of Hitler, is lying in the Radcliffe Infirmary. *Oxford Mail*, Saturday 27th January 1940.

Censorship during the war only permitted the newspapers to report the mid-January 1940 freeze-up in Oxford, the worst experienced in Oxford since 1895, a fortnight after it had happened. Pictures below show both the Isis and the Cherwell rivers frozen over.

---

[20] Hugh Cairns rowed at Bow for Oxford in the 1920 Boat Race. He is best remembered for treating T.E. Lawrence after his eventually fatal motorcycle accident and for his research that led to both military and civilian use of crash helmets for motorcycle riders. The Library at the John Radcliffe, part of the Bodleian Library, is named after him.

Oxford's Biggest Frost Since 1895. *Oxford Mail*, Monday 29th January 1940

[late January or early February] 1940

Dear Mother and Father,

Today, I am enclosing as many of the films that came out. They are numbered to distinguish them:-

1. 'Dopey' Donaldson

2. Magdalen Tower from the 'Spit'[21].

---

[21] The Spit is the small peninsular strip of school land that protrudes from the south side of Magdalen Bridge, surrounded by two courses of the River Cherwell and reached by crossing the first white bridge.

3. 2nd bridge with Lyndon ma.

4. 'The Spit'

5. Magdalen Tower from 'Ma – d's garden.[22]

6. Magdalen and Botanical gardens from the playfield.

The negative half blotched over is Metcalf. I do hope you like my little present. Donaldson says he is willing to buy his photo if it is enlarged. Unfortunately the price for the films is too much for me, being 1/6, so I hope to get them on credit. Perhaps I'll write later in the week to tell you any bits and bobs of news which I can pick up,

Your loving son, Michael.

Stop – Press. The Lyndons are taking me out to tea today.[23]

Such was its impact, the big freeze of late January 1940 continued to be written about in local newspapers for several weeks after the thaw, with 8th and 10th February editions of the *Oxford Mail* giving memorable headlines and some of the most charming and captivating images of the time.

HOW THE GREAT BLIZZARD HIT OXFORD. CLIMAX OF JANUARY'S MEMORABLE FROST. Rail and Road Hold-Up: Villages Isolated; Littlemore Without Drinking Water. *Oxford Mail*, Thursday 8th February 1940

---

[22] The Master, Rushworth Kennard Davis, was known as 'Pa D', his wife was referred to as 'Ma D'.

[23] Permission to go out with friends' parents or even your own parents or relatives at weekends had to be asked for in advance and was not always given.

St Aldate's in a Christmas Card setting, with the snowploughs at work clearing the streets after one of the heaviest falls in recent years. *Oxford Mail*, Thursday 8th February 1940

The 'Saga' on the Cherwell, below, was poignantly a group of Michael's fellow MCS boarders floating on 'ice-bergs' close by to School House and in sight of the famous white bridges.[24]

---

[24] The white bridges link the school and its boarding house to the school field which is a island in the River Cherwell.

SAGA OF THE GREAT WHITE RIVER (CHERWELL) *Oxford Mail*, Saturday 10th February 1940

Chapter I. Marooned as we were in the wastes of that bitter land, with our boats gone and no weapons to hand but our pick-axes and broken oars, what could we do but cut one of the ice-floes into the form of a raft and entrust ourselves to it in the faith that it would carry us back to civilisation? It was our last desperate hope

Chapter II. At last, after seemingly endless toil, our raft was finished, and, having swept it with delicate care, we raised a little cheer as we launched it into the great white river, for on its slippery back rested all our hopes. Originally our little party numbered six, but, at the last moment, a younger member of the community stepped aboard and in spite of all the protests, could not be dislodged before it was too late. He stands in the foreground in an overcoat.

Chapter III. Alas, it was not long before all hands had to go to work in an effort to save our improvised craft from foundering. As it lurched on the water, our only hope was to cut off its corners in the hope of saving the central platform.

Chapter IV. All our efforts proved unavailing, and, with a deathly crack, the raft began to break. Before we could even say a prayer or make our peace with the spirits of the Arctic, into these icy waters we were all plunged. What terrors waited us there, what hidden monsters waited for their pray? Only the future could tell.

The episode was prompted by the boy's impatience to launch the boats for the first time in the rowing term, the river having been ice-bound since the start of the year.

[Sunday 18th February] 1940

Dear Mother and Father,

Thank you both very much for the 3/- P.O you sent me, and the torch.

I was absent from school for 2 days this week, with the result that I was 5th in form. In answer to your question about the population of our form, it is about 20.

Pitts wants to know what I am to do when I run out of Cod liver oil and malt.

Now I have run out of grub so will you please send me a tin of toffee, some digestive biscuits, and some nice lemon cheese cakes like those we had at our Xmas party.

Also could you please send some more stamp hinges and a good packet of British stamps.

The other day I saw hundreds of troops and several tanks proceeding along xxxx street.[25]

---

[25] Michael thoughtfully censored his own letter, and didn't give away the street name along which the troop movement proceeded. However, proximity to school and with four x's it is likely to have been High Street.

This week Ivor Novello[26] in person is at the New Theatre[27] so can you please send enough money to go and see him; or do you think that I could get a good seat free if I said that you had known him in youth.

Last night we had 'In Exitu Israel' in chapel, and I thought it was simply grand.

Your loving son, Michael

Ivor Novello Play at New Theatre. *Oxford Mail*, Saturday 17th February 1940

---

[26] Ivor Novello was an old boy and ex-chorister of MCS. Michael wanted to see the new play by Novello called *Second Helping*, which ran for one week starting on Monday 19th February 1939. Before each performance of the play, in which Novello played Lord Justin Perrivale, Novello entertained with a 'Song Parade', containing excerpts from his song hits from his Drury Lane successes. The following week Novello's play *Full House*, with its full cast from the Haymarket Theatre in London, came to the New Theatre.

[27] Theatres and cinemas in Oxford, like the rest of the UK, had briefly closed down at the outbreak of war but were reopened again just two weeks later in mid-September 1939.

[February] 1940

Dear Mother and Father,

Thank you both very much for the stamps and hinges. Could you please send a 2½d stamp for my British collection.

The price of the photos was 1/6. If you please send money for another roll of film, I'll take a photo of the field in flood, as it is now over 3 ft. deep, and the Boat Club is using tub pairs and what not on what was once dry land.[28] This week I am top of form I.

I'll be writing again next Friday, which is the most convenient day of the week for letter writing.

Your loving son, Michael.

The floods in Oxford during February 1940 that Michael mentions in his letter home is evident in this picture of the 1940 Torpids races on the Isis.

OPENING OF THE OXFORD UNIVERSITY WAR-TIME TORPIDS. Close Racing in the Gut in Division II race of the Oxford University Torpids shows the flooding and broken banks of the Isis. *Oxford Mail*, Thursday 22nd February 1940

---

[28] The school's magazine, *The Lily* of March 1940, reporting on the first three months of 1940, stated that 'For three long weeks the river froze and with the thaws the waters covered the field.'

[February] 1940

Dear Mother and Father,

I'm afraid that I haven't written to Aunty Berny yet, but I'll try on Saturday or Sunday.

I hope I'm not asking for too much but do you think it would be possible to get me 'Inside Knowledge', it is obtainable at Smith's.

Thank you very much for the magazine which you sent me, it is very interesting.

Can you please send me the story of the 'Cossack'.

Please could you send me 9d to see a picture at the 'Super'.[29] I was very surprised when our 1st IV beat Magdalen College 1st IV by 1¼ lengths. Donaldson, who coxes the 1st IV has got his coxing colours.

Your loving son, Michael

While the country suffered from the aftermath of the floods caused by the big freeze, the story which Michael requested his parents to send, concerning the Tribal-class destroyer HMS Cossack, captivated the nation. The Cossack became famous for the boarding of the German supply ship Altmark in Norwegian waters on 16th February 1940, and the associated rescue of sailors originally captured by the Admiral Graf Spee. During the episode 299 prisoners were freed, while seven crew members of the German ship were killed. HMS Cossack was eventually torpedoed by U-563 and sank on 27th October 1941.

BRITISH PRISONERS RESCUED. Graf Spee Supply Ship Intercepted By Warships.
Oxford Mail, Saturday 17th February 1940

---

[29] The Oxford 'Super' Cinema is now the Odeon on Magdalen Street, Oxford.

[late February] 1940

'Somewhere in England'

Dear Mother and Father,

Thank you very much for the cakes and digestive biscuits, and the map which I received today.

I'm sorry that I didn't write before now.

The rugger match was very exciting, despite a very hot day. Oxford's best man was No.5, and their worst was No.6. The Oxford full-back broke his nose. This week I am 5th in form.

Will you please send me some marbles? because this is the marble term.

No news this week.

Your loving Michael

Sporting life at both Oxford and Cambridge Universities attempted to carry on as normal despite the war.

CAMBRIDGE SCORE ELEVEN POINTS IN SIX MINUTES TO BEAT OXFORD. Rugby report and pictures of Oxford's 'very exciting' 14 – 13 loss to Cambridge, played at Iffley Road. *Oxford Mail*, Saturday 24th February and Monday 26th February 1940.

Left, **THIS IS BOAT RACE DAY.** Right, **How Oxford finished to-day's Boat Race at Henley – five lengths behind Cambridge.** *Oxford Mail*, Saturday 2nd March 1940.

[Sunday] 3rd March 1940

Dear Mother and Father,

I'm afraid I can't write about much this week, but here are some films to develop. When they are developed will you please send them back so that I can identify them for you.

Thank you very much for the parcel, which I received yesterday.

I am very sorry that Oxford lost the boat race.[30]

Yesterday I went to see a hockey match between our 1st XI and the Old boys; they won 5-0.[31]

Your loving son, Michael.

PS. What do you think of the 'Cossack'?

---

[30] This was the first of the four unofficial boat races held during the Second World War away from London. In 1940 and 1945 the race was held at Henley-on-Thames; in 1943 it was held at Sandford-on-Thames; and in 1944 it was held on the Great Ouse River, from Ely, Littleport to Queen Adelaide. As none of those competing were awarded blues, these races are not included in the Boat Race official list. On 2 March 1940, a considerably more experienced and weighty Cambridge crew beat Oxford.

[31] The Old Boy side actually beat the School 7-0. The modern-day school now refers to its alumni as Old Waynflete's, or OW's, after the school's founder William Waynflete.

Michael's pictures of HMS Cossack and The Altmark, drawn at the end of his 3rd March 1940 letter.

The Hilary term at MCS, January to April, was hockey season and many of the fixtures played by the school were against college and other adult sides, like the Old Boys mentioned in Michael's previous letter and the City of Oxford Hockey Club depicted in the *Oxford Mail*, see below. For modern players it is interesting to note the old 'English style' sticks being used.

SECOND LIEUTENANT P. BICKERTON[32] (white shirt) making a shot at goal while playing for City of Oxford Hockey Club against Magdalen College School. *Oxford Mail*, Monday 18th March 1940.

---

[32] Second Lieutenant P. L. Bickerton was an Old Waynflete, serving with the Royal Artillery.

The British Governments campaign warning the public to take precautions against potential spies, 'Careless Talk Costs Lives', brought much paranoia to the country. Even Michael was doing his part, choosing only to disclose his location as 'Somewhere in England' in his correspondance of February 1940. In Oxford, Boars Hill, simple inquisitiveness about a crashed plane ended in an Austrian undergraduate student at Lincoln College, Wilhelm Solf being first imprisoned and finally interned for the duration of the war.

SOLF SENT TO INTERNMENT CAMP. SECRET RELEASE FROM THE OXFORD PRISON.
The Home Secretary (Sir John Anderson) has decided that Wilhelm Solf, living until a month ago at Boars Hill, Oxford, shall be interned. Solf, ex-German cavalryman and aircraft worker, and until recently a member of Lincoln College, Oxford, was sent to prison for a month by the Abingdon Magistrates for infringing the regulations in photographing an aircraft wreck at Boars Hill. *Oxford Mail*, Monday 25th March 1940.

Summer (Trinity) Term 1940

As the summer term of 1940 got underway, the 'Phoney War' was about to come to an abrupt end, the British Army would soon be cornered in France and forced to make a hasty retreat from the French coast in a hotchpotch flotilla of small boats and navy vessels, epitomised by the scenes at Dunkirk. Meanwhile, in Oxford during the lead-up to these monumental times the atmosphere in the city at night was described as a 'Bear Garden', with adolescents enjoying life to the full, making a nuisance of themselves and seemingly oblivious to what was unfolding across the Channel. Indeed, despite defence exercises taking place in and around the city, life in Oxford carried on as normal, with the usual festivities and crowds at the foot of Magdalen Tower and on Magdalen Bridge on May Morning.

'Oxford Is Like A Bear Garden At Night'. **Social Education Till 18 Advocated.** Mr Eric Roberts, joint secretary of the Oxford Youth Organisations Committee said that he was appalled by the increase in loafing by young people in Oxford. 'Crowds of youths and girls spent their evenings walking up and down the streets or gathering on corners, whistling, shouting, singing and screaming, and rendering Oxford after dark more like a bear garden than a beautiful city.' *Oxford Mail*, Monday 15th April 1940.

OXFORD COTTAGES SET ON FIRE FOR A.R.P. City and District Co-operate in large-scale excercises. Between 2,000 and 3,000 Oxford A.R.P. workers went into action yesterday afternoon in the Southern defence exercise, the most ambitious and extensive Oxford has so far undertaken. For nearly four hours nearly the whole of Oxford's A.R.P. services, assisted by reinforcements from Oxfordshire and Berkshire were operating. **MAGDALEN BRIDGE INVOLVED** 'Magdalen Bridge was assumed to have been destroyed and the casualties totalled 50.' '... two cottages in Marston

Road near Jack Straw's Lane were fired and there the Oxford Fire Brigade received the assistance of the Abingdon Fire Brigade.' '... these fires attracted considerable interest.' 'Soldiers in battle dress, with rifles and fixed bayonets, were brought to the scene to stand by and control the crowds.' *Oxford Mail*, Monday 29th April 1940.

OXFORD MAY MORNING CEREMONY
Above: Magdalen College Choir singing the traditional Latin hymns on the top of Magdalen College tower this morning. Right: Looking down from the top of Magdalen College Tower on the crowd on Magdalen Bridge and in punts on the Cherwell at 6am to-day, when the traditional May-morning ceremony was observed. *Oxford Mail*, Wednesday 1st May 1940.

[Sunday 5th May] 1940

Dear Mater and Pater,

Well, I had a glorious May-day. We got up at 5, started singing at 6.30, (in the college) and spent 1½ hours in a punt, at the expense of the college. After that it was a choir-practice, and at 10.30 we were back at school.[33]

This week 'Gulliver's travels' is coming to the 'Regal',[34] so please can you send me a P.O. as I'm stoney broke.

I've been doing some good drawings this week and soon I'll be sending one of them.

I have not received the stamps yet. This week I was 6th in form.

Yours, 'Funf'[35].

where is 'FUNF?' Advertisement for James Russell & Co. of 120 High Street, Oxford, who sold amongst other things, radios. Here they are using the 'It's that man again' radio character 'Funf' in their advert.
The Oxford Times, 1940.

GULLIVER'S TRAVELS. *The Oxford Times*, Friday 3rd May 1940.

---

[33] Choir rehearsal was in the practice room of the main quadrangle of Magdalen College and until 1941 was taken by Dr William Mckie. In the first term Michael was 'overwhelmed by the full-throated first entry into Stanford' after 'the rather uncertain singing at St Paul's in Stafford.' The sound was 'something amazing and new, a full professional sound such as I never dreamt of.'

[34] The 'Regal', 300 Cowley Road, East Oxford, is no longer a cinema but the building survives and is Grade II listed.

[35] Michael uses the name 'Funf' for himself only once in his letters home. He did sign 'Shirley' in small writing at the bottom of the letter. Funf was the German spy character on the BBC radio comedy programme of the time, 'It's That Man Again'. Spoken by Jack Train, 'This is Funf speaking' became a popular telephone catchphrase and was also briefly adopted by many as a comical nickname.

On the evening of Wednesday 1st May 1940, a secret ambush and demonstration, mainly by students against a May Day workers' procession, organised by the Oxford Trades Council, turned into what the *Oxford Mail* described as 'the most amazing night which Oxford has ever witnessed'. The procession, which also included the Oxford branch of the Communist Party, the Oxford City Labour Party, the Oxford Unemployed Association and some undergraduate sympathisers called for equal opportunities and rights for all, university places for all and higher wages. The Oxford Communist Party believed they were the chief target of the demonstrators who were mainly made up of students.

Undergraduates In Oxford Street 'War'. *Oxford Mail*, Thursday 2nd May 1940.

The *Oxford Mail* reported 'Oxford has never witnessed such amazing scenes as those which took place last night when an organised and lively demonstration, which had been kept a closely guarded secret until the actual 'outbreak of hostilities', was launched against the May Day procession.

During the fray tomatoes, apples, oranges, eggs, streams of liquid from soda syphons, bags of flour and homemade fireworks were showered upon the procession by undergraduates, who lined the route from The Plain to St Giles and who crowded into windows of University lodging houses.'

OXFORD MAY DAY 'RIOT'. Wild scenes were witnessed in Oxford last night when a May Day procession organised by the Oxford Trades Council was subjected to a hostile demonstration by undergraduates. Photograph above shows the opening of hostilities in the High Street. Members of the procession are seen picking up missiles to return fire and leaving the ranks to attack their tormentors.

IN ST. GILES — Speaker trying to get a hearing.
Oxford Mail, Thursday 2nd May 1940

The following run of headlines from the *Oxford Mail* during the summer term of 1940, depicts the rapid development of hostilities in Europe during May 1940 and helps to conjure up the likely emotions and feelings of the Oxford population, as well as the nation at the time.

HOLLAND, BELGIUM AND LUXEMBURG INVADED.
Oxford Mail, Friday 10th May 1940.

OUR AIM IS VICTORY – MR. CHURCHILL. *Oxford Mail*, Monday 13th May 1940.

GERMANS OCCUPY ARRAS AND AMIENS. *Oxford Mail*, Tuesday 21st May 1940.

GERMANS REACH BOULOGNE. *Oxford Mail*, Thursday 23rd May 1940.

THREE BOMBING RAIDS ON ENGLAND. *Oxford Mail*, Saturday 25th May 1940.

B.E.F. WITHDRAWS NEARER COAST. *Oxford Mail*, Wednesday 29th May 1940.

BELGIAN ARMY CAPITULATES. *Oxford Mail*, Tuesday 28th May 1940.

DUNKIRK STILL HELD BY ALLIES. *Oxford Mail*, Friday 31st May 1940.

Meanwhile, no matter the inner anxieties and emotions, the public and student population of Oxford attempted to carry on their routines as normal and or at least as best as possible.

A grandstand view of the Oxford Summer Eights from the new bridge over the Isis during yesterday's Division III race. *Oxford Mail*, Friday 24th May 1940.

At the athletic meeting between Oxford Y.M.C.A and Magdalen College School yesterday: L. Keen (Magdalen C.S.) winning the mile race. *Oxford Mail*, Friday 31st May 1940.

N.T.A. Fiennes (who made 157) and S.I. Phillips (who made 178) going out to bat for Oxford University against the British Empire XI on the Christ Church ground at Oxford. *Oxford Mail*, Saturday 15th June 1940.

After two terms at his new school, Michael's attempt to win acceptance of his preferred, second name for everyday use comes to an abrupt end and he resigns to signing himself by his first name, Shirley, the name his parents and family then used when addressing him. His reversion and acquiescence to signing himself Shirley continues for the next five and a half years, until the dawn of 1946. Only once turned sixteen and with a new world order, would Michael find the inner confidence to revert to his preferred name as his signature name.

[early May] 1940

Dear Mother and Father,

Thanks very much for the Jugoslavia stamps that you sent me. They filled 1½ pages.

I'm in a rather bad mood today, because Mr Davis wouldn't give me perm. to see 'Gulliver's Travels', which was a picture that I wanted to see for quiete [quite] a long time.

On Sunday Mr Mackie [Mckie] is going to take me up the Tower to take a photo if it's a fine day, so will you please send me a roll of film, together with a pkt. of those 'Chocolate Imperials', and one or two packets of digestive biscuits.

This week Mr Lomas, the great bass came to visit us. He is 73. Also, a certain Mr. Cocker came to see us, and he says he remembers you 'By the same mop of hair'; I believe he was music master.

Yours, Shirley.

P.S. Will you please send me the ½d, 1½d and 3d ones of the new stamps.

This pencil drawing by Michael was included in this letter home. On the reverse he wrote: 'Looking toward Cowley from the Tower' – Michael Hickey, aged 10.

Central in the drawing is Magdalen Bridge, leading to The Plain. Protruding from the second line of Poplar trees is the School boarding house with its small cupula.

[May or June] 1940

Dear Mother and Father,

Thank you very much for the parcel that you sent me. The stamps on it had not been touched; they were perfectly unused.

Someone has stolen some English stamps from my album, so that I am now going to keep it locked. The stamps were the new 2d, and the old 2½d, 8d, 9d, and 1/-. I can now swim 3 quarters of a width at the baths,[36] which are very modern.[37]

The heat at present is tropical[38] as I lie on the field with a boy called Lawther.

I am looking now at some boys who have taken plots of ground on the outskirts of the field and have planted various vegetables.

Yours, Shirley.

Ink drawing of Shirley Temple by Michael that appeared at the end of this letter.

OXFORD'S 'SHIRLEY TEMPLE'. Shirley Temple was such a popular and well-known Hollywood star at the time that it was common to refer to any promising young girl singer or actress as the local Shirley Temple. Indeed, this headline appeared when, in 1942 a young girl known as 'Oxford's Shirley Temple' was knocked down and injured by a lorry on the Iffley Road near by the school. *Oxford Mail*, Saturday 6th June 1942

---

[36] Being able to swim 25 yards (known at the time as the 'short pass') was Michael's main aim, as according to the school rules this would allow him to go beyond the five-yard distance from the river that none swimmers had to stick to, an important consideration for boarders living on the banks of the Cherwell and wanting to explore along its many streams and islands. Once a 50 yard swim could be accomplished, boys were also allowed to swim at the bathing point on School Field. Mr Rathbone and the Geography teacher Mr Insley were delegated the task of teaching the boys to swim.

[37] The 'very modern' baths were Temple Cowley Baths, opened in 1938. Two miles away from MCS, visits to the Baths were a half hour walk.

[38] A sixteen day drought in the run up to the Sports Days of 1940 (Thursday 13th and Saturday 15th June 1940) had produced a very hard baked School Field.

In addition to using the extremities of School Field to grow vegetables and supplement the food rations, the narrow area of land between the '1928' teaching block and Cowley Place was divided in to small allotments and boys were encouraged to 'Dig for Victory'. Cultivation of park land and playing fields became a common sight throughout Oxford and other towns during the war and even the sacred University Parks were utilised for allotments.

ALLOTMENTS IN OXFORD UNIVERSITY PARKS: Members of the Co-operative War Allotments Corps at work on an acre of ground in the University Parks, Oxford, which has been leased to them. On right, Mrs. Lobel, a doughty founder of the corps. *Oxford Mail*, Wednesday 27th November 1940.

The school held competitions for growing the largest vegetables and one year, as measurement day neared for the largest marrow competition, it was noted that Mr Elam's marrow was by far the largest. One night before the judging day, the prize marrow disappeared. It is rumoured that one of the boys sent it floating down the Cherwell!

Monday 27th May 1940

Dear Mummy and Daddy,

I am writing yet again to tell you that on the night I last wrote we had a terribly long raid, which lasted 4 hours. I went to sleep while I was down there,[39] and while I was in dreamland, the blinkin' Jerries were bombing Bicester. The concussion of the bombs and AA fire was tremendous.

Nowadays the river is swarming with good-sized perch, and at least 10 boys have got fishing rods, which only cost 2/1½d. If you were kind enough to send me some money to buy a rod I will be very thankful to you. Metcalfe has landed 4 or 5 perch during the last three days, and, with a bit of practice I will be able to catch some fish.

I will not be writing on Sunday as all my news is contained in these letters.

Yours lovingingly [lovingly], Shirley

*Michael's drawing of a British Tommy[40] that appeared at
the end of his letter of 27th May 1940.*

---

[39] When the siren sounded the young boys had to go to the school library in the basement of School House, the older boys went to the Dining Hall. In these 'safe' locations were paillasses that the boys slept/rested on until the all clear was sounded.
[40] Tommy Atkins, often just Tommy, is slang for a common soldier in the British Army. It is particularly associated with the First World War but was also used frequently in the Second World War.

British Tommies were a familiar sight in Oxford during the summer of 1940 and Michael remembered how during the time of Dunkirk 'we had gazed in amazement as [for two days] columns of exhausted troops marched across Magdalen Bridge, in transit from barracks at Cowley, where they had presumably been fed and watered, and on to trains taking them all over the country where they would have been cleaned up, issued with new uniforms and weapons, [some of them were wearing French helmets, some of them were in mixed dress, none of them or very few were armed] and assigned to their units as the nation prepared itself for German invasion.' As during the Great War, the University Examination Schools on the High Street were commandeered as a military hospital and its convalescent patients, clad in ill-fitting blue uniforms and red neckties, wandered freely around Oxford.

[June] 1940

Dear Mummy and Daddy,

I'm sorry I have not written before and about that letter business. On Monday I was in bed all day with indigestion.

Thank you very much for the P.O., but I am afraid it was sent in vain, for I discovered that the boy's father had sold the rod for 7/6d. However, I think he is giving me another as my old one is all tangled at the top and one of the sections is bust. The other week I had an amusing adventure with a dead dace. You see, I had been fishing with a boy, who caught this fish, and he let me keep it in my tackle tin; after that I forgot about it for at least a fortnight, when I noticed that a vile stink was issuing from the tin: I opened it, and there was this dead fish! I put on my gas-mask, as I was nearly sick with the smell and another boy and myself conveyed the vile smell out of the changing room.

During the last 3 weeks Mr Davis has been reading to our form a book by his son called 'Isle of Adventure'[41] and he said that I could have [it] on my bill at the end of term with your perm[mission].

Your loving son. Shirley.

---

[41] *Isle of Adventure* written by A.S. Kennard Davis was published in 1937 by Basil Blackwell, Oxford.

[Sunday 9th June] 1940

Dear Mummy and Daddy,

I'm terribly sorry that I am writing in pencil this week, but the only ink I could get hold of was invisible ink.

When you come on Friday you will hear in chapel 'Why do the heathen so furiously rage together' by Mendollsohn [Mendelssohn], and the service is Travers in A.

Well, now about news; item No. 1. I've got an awful boil but Pitts is attending to it two or three times per day.

In answer to your question about grub, I would like a sponge; some of those lemon cheese cakes; some pkts of chocolate biscuits and some digestive biscuits together with a roll of films for my camera. I'll tell all the other news on Friday.

Yours, Shirley

On the same day that France's capitulation was announced in the *Oxford Mail* and Churchill's announcement that Britain will fight on until victory is won, Monday 17th June 1940, the paper reported on the MCS Commemoration and Prize Giving Day and the importance of the current school boys as the future leaders and world builders. Quoting the speaker at the Prize Giving, the headmaster of Uppingham advised the boys to 'look about five years ahead when a burden would be laid on them which they would not be able to escape.'

Britain Will Fight On Until Victory Is Won. FRANCE GIVES UP THE FIGHT.
Oxford Mail, Monday 17th June 1940

Left: **SCHOOLBOYS AS NEW WORLD LEADERS**. Importance Stressed at Magdalen College School Commemoration. Right: **Evacuees arriving at Banbury on Saturday.** *Oxford Mail*, Monday 17th June 1940.

During the fraught summer of 1940 when an airborne invasion by Germany appeared imminent, senior boys of the school's OTC were put on duty each night with rifles and fixed bayonets, but no ammunition, defending Magdalen Bridge. A tent was pitched on the Spit, beside the first white bridge as a make shift guard room. The boys returned to their dorms at first light to grab some sleep. Other senior boys who weren't guarding Magdalen Bridge would be on night-time fire watching duty, sleeping on camp beds in the bicycle shed in the summer and in the old 3rd Form room (a wooden hut that had originally been at Magdalen College) in the winter months. At first light these boys would have a quick swim at Milham Ford before turning in. Being 'under orders', a blind eye was turned when, during the day they finally succumbed to tiredness and dropped off in their lessons.

Tuesday 25th June 1940

Dear Mummy and Daddy,

I am writing you a hasty note to tell you that early this morning, at 1 a.m. the sirens went, as the Jerries who were on their way to Cardiff etc came over Oxford. This is how it happened. I was dozing in bed when suddenly and eerily a very familiar sound came to my ears – f f f f f f f , so I immediately got out of bed and woke up the prefect with the words 'Quick Smith, it's an air-raid'. He told me to stand by and await orders, while the others woke up one by one. We all slipped on our trousers, put on our slippers, and grabbed a blanket. Instead of using the stuffy library, we used the dining hall.[42] Everyone was splendidly calm and cheerful. Cornell and Stephens (our second head chorister) played the piano and we all had a singsong, consisting mainly of 'In the Quarter Masters Stores' and 'What shall we do with the drunken sailor'. Towards the end Stephens played some of his own music, as he takes music.

At 1.50 a.m. the 'All Clear' came through and we all dashed happily upstairs.

By the way when we went downstairs to the dining hall we wore our dressing gowns.

You loving son, Shirley

P.S. I am anxious to withdraw the caption about a 'hasty note' at the beginning as it is now a miniature volume.

Later the same day, the *Oxford Mail* published reports of the first extensive air raids on Britain, but for censorship reasons did not specify the effected town(s), in this report only referring to 'a south-west English town'.

Five Feared Dead in Raid: Wrecked House Search. 14 Badly hurt also in S.W. town.
Oxford Mail, Tuesday 25th June 1940.

---

[42] After many false alarms Michael recalled that the boarders were eventually seldom called from their beds when the sirens went.

The German air-raids of June and July 1940 were small probing attacks made to test the British defences and to give German aircrew experience of both day and night bombing over Britain. In July and August, the Luftwaffe focused on destroying the RAF as a fighting force and attacking its supply lines. By late August, believing the RAF was close to defeat, the Luftwaffe switched to attacking military and industrial targets around London and other parts of Britain. The heavy raids on London, in particular the dock area, began on 7th September and continued for almost four months. In November the focus of the attacks moved away from London to other major cities and ports. Then in the spring of 1941 the campaign diverted its attention to focus on the major ports. The end of this sustained campaign of bombing, now referred to as The Blitz, came with a final major raid on London on 10th and 11th May 1941.

Tuesday 9th July [1940]

Dear Mother, Father, 'Bishy', 'Sinner' and 'Vaccy'[43],

I am writing this letter to thank M & D for their letters, which I thought were very nice.

I have got two troubles; one is that mummy sent the wrong kind of 2d stamp, and that the hook of my rod is broken, and I'm waiting till I get home before I start fishing. I think the best place is Trentham, but, of course you're not allowed out of the town, and we can't fish at Acton Trussell, as some fishing club owns everything.

I'm afraid that I've lost the letter with Uncle's address in it, so will you please send it again, with a NEW SERIES 2d unused stamp.

I've got some lovely Spanish stamps now and also 4 beautiful Bulgarian stamps. Also I have over 980 stamps in my collection and you can guess that my album is rather crowded, so please may I choose another album for the holidays; my suggestion is 'Triumph' stamp album. It has got spaces for over 16,000 stamps, and there are also

---

[43] It is not known who Vaccy was.

ten good maps in front; another blessing is that spare pages can be inserted.

I am glad that the girls enjoyed Stafford Castle; please can you take me there this vac?

Another question I want to ask is that: <u>will I be evacuated to Canada</u>? If they make the feeblest sign of taking me to Canada I will flatly refuse, as I would be much happier in England, with bombs dropping than in a British colony on a rainy day. So shucks-boo to any drydist [?] official who tries to evacuate <u>ME</u>.[44]

Have you heard that Hitler is going to raid England tomorrow (the 10th)? If he does he'll have a kick-in-the-pants that he'll never forget.

Your loving son, Shirley.

[July] 1940

Dear Mummy and Daddy,

This week I'm afraid I'm writing on a Tuesday. Exams are in full progress, and so far I have been top in Latin and maths. The other week I came top in form order, so I'm expecting a good report.

But now come[s] bad news. I'm afraid that I'll have to leave my tuck-box at school this time, as the thing has been forced, and I can't even fasten it.

The best plan is that a new tuck-box will have to be bought.

---

[44] Between June and September 1940, the Children's Overseas Reception Board organised and facilitated the evacuation of 1,532 children to Canada. In total the CORB approved 24,000 children for evacuation overseas to British Colonies, but the scheme was cancelled after the SS City of Benares was torpedoed on 17 September 1940 while on its way to Canada, killing 77 of the 90 CORB children aboard. Overseas evacuation of children did continue by private endeavours, including 6,000 to Canada.

I am looking forward to coming home, so that I can see the girls[45] and 'Vaccy'.

Your loving son, Shirley

P.S. Will you please quickly send me some money as we are getting Pitts a present as she is leaving, or shall I put it on the bill[?] S.M.H.

Michael (centre) with the two evacuee girls from Ramsgate, Diana Saint[46] and Joan (?)[47], billeted with Michael's parents at 45 Rising Brook, Stafford.

---

[45] The girls that Michael mentions are Diana and Joan, two evacuees from Ramsgate in Kent who were billeted with Michael's parents at 45 Rising Brook. In June 1940, as the threat of invasion by the Germans loomed, over three thousand children were evacuated from Ramsgate, the majority were taken to Staffordshire for billets. After the threat of invasion diminished in 1941 and 1942, many of the children began to return to Ramsgate.

[46] Diana's surname is revealed on the back of this photo as Saint, hence Michael's nickname for her, 'Sinner'.

[47] Joan's surname was not written on the back of the photo, but Michael's nickname for her, 'Bishy', and records from the time indicate that this is likely to be Joan Margaret Bish.

Autumn 1940 – Summer 1941

May Day, Music and Flight Path to Coventry

During the Second World War, the National Savings Movement was transformed by the War Office into a War Savings Campaign to support the war effort. Local savings weeks were held which were promoted with posters and titles such as 'Save your way to Victory' and 'War Savings are Warships'.

OXFORD'S WAR SAVINGS BAROMETER on Carfax Tower shows that savings are steadily rising towards the £2,500,000 mark. *Oxford Mail*, Friday 27th September 1940.

Autumn (Michaelmas) Term 1940

During this term the school groundsman, Mr William Collett, 'Pro', was called up for Military Service. The captains of games (ie. the 1st team captains of Rugby, Hockey and Cricket) were therefore made responsible for the upkeep of the playing field. William Collett

returned to the school in 1946 and worked as the groundsman until his retirement in the summer of 1978, having joined the school some fifty years earlier in 1928.

Friday 20th September 1940

Dear Mummy and Daddy,

This afternoon I was fishing off the two bridges, but as I've got no decent tackle, I couldn't hold my fish when I struck, so could you send me some tackle?

Yesterday I was three hours late arriving at Oxford and it was nearly tea-time when I arrived at the school-house.

It might be possible for Taylor and myself to come back together at the end of term. Taylor and myself are in command of Middle Little study.

Well goodbye and give my love (with knobs on) to the girls.

Love from Shirley.

P.S. IT'S THE LIBRARY AUCTION TONIGHT AFTER SUPPER STATES REUTER[48].

These three caricatures of the two evacuees and Michael's self-portrait appeared at the end of Michael's letter of 20th September 1940.

---

[48] It is not known who Reuter was.

Although Oxford was to eventually come through the war without being bombed, no one during that time assumed that would be the case and planning for a bombing raid, considered an eventuality, continued incessantly. A constant reminder to the school boys at MCS that Oxford could be heavily bombed was the location and presence of the Oxford Rescue Squad and a Public Air-Raid shelter on school land at The Plain, off the Iffley Road.

If Oxford Is Heavily Bombed: City's Plans For Prompt Relief. Schools Earmarked as Rest Homes. Specific schools[49] across Oxford were earmarked as 'rest centres' in the event of people being bombed out of their homes. To be run by members of the Women's Volunteer Service, residents were to be provided with iron rations[50] and shelter until arrangements to live with relatives or friends were made. *Oxford Mail*, Thursday 3rd October 1940.

---

[49] MCS was not one of the twelve designated 'Rest Centres', but two nearby schools which were assigned for this purpose included Milham Ford School, then recently moved to the Marston Road, and East Oxford Council School on Union Street.

[50] Iron rations are an emergency ration, typically a preserved meat, cheese, biscuit, tea, sugar and salt for use in the event of their being cut off from regular food supplies.

Members of the Oxford City A.R.P. Rescue Squad who were inspected by the Mayor of Oxford and other members of the Council at their Depot. *Oxford Mail*, Tuesday 15th October 1940.

SURELY NOT! 'Boats To Let' is the notice to be found at the entrance to this air-raid shelter at The Plain at Oxford. *Oxford Mail*, Tuesday 15th October 1940. [In the background of this picture is School House, the boarding house where Michael lived and its Cowley Place entrance]

[Autumn] 1940

Dear Mummy and Daddy,

This term we have had 3 air-raid warnings one during Prep. on Friday night, the second on Sunday and the third today.[51]

Yesterday I was at tea with Mrs Rutherford, and whilst I was there the syr<u>eeeee</u>ns went.

Today I was packing up my fishing at 4.55p.m. when the syr<u>eeeeeeeeeeeeee</u>ns went; after putting on my skin again I went up into the schoolhouse and had tea, the raid lasted for about 25 minutes.

I am improving in French, but Latin is about the same, as our Latin master – well, he's just gross.

Yours everlastingly friend,

Shirley (A.F.) (L.M.S.)

Michael again drew cartoons of Bishy and Sinner at the end of this letter. He also signed his name, Shirley, in an uncharacteristic style (possibly written left handed). Post-nominal letters were included after each name, but it is not known what these stood for.

---

[51] It is possible that the day-light reconnaissance photograph of Oxford, taken by the German's on 24th September 1940 and seen later in this book, was taken during one of these air-raids.

The Government encouraged universities to continue their educational efforts as best as possible, despite the war and the decrease in student numbers. In the newspaper report of 3rd October 1940 below, Professor George Gordon (President of Magdalen College, 1928-42 and Vice-Chancellor of Oxford University, 1938-1941) reported that Lord Halifax (Foreign Secretary 1938-40 and Chancellor of Oxford University 1933-59) and the Government's wish was that Universities should continue their educational work and tutoring of students. At the same time, as can be seen later in the newspaper report of the *Oxford Mail* of 16th November, student membership of the University's cadet corps was also encouraged, enabling students to be fast tracked into military service if needed.

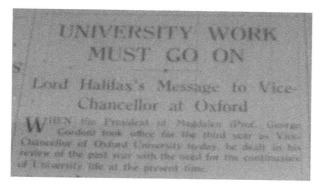

UNIVERSITY WORK MUST GO ON. Lord Halifax's Message to Vice Chancellor at Oxford. *Oxford Mail*, Thursday 3rd October 1940.

If the universities' job was to carry on as normal, the public's job was to save. Starting on 30th November 1940, Oxford held its first 'War Weapons Week' encouraging the public to take out war savings bonds to help generate money for weapons manufacture. These focused and themed (Salute the Soldier week, Wings for Victory week, etc) savings weeks continued periodically throughout the war and brought many military attractions to towns and cities that not only motivated adults to be patriotic and save, but also captivated the imagination of young school children such as Michael. Newspapers at the time ran articles and advertisements to encourage participation in these events.

Oxford War Weapons Week, November 30th to December 7th 1940. Organised by the Oxford Saving's Committee.

The German bomber which will be on view in Oxford during War Weapons Week being assembled in St Giles'.

Oxford Mail, Thursday 28th November 1940

Oxford Has Its Biggest Parade. Weapons Week Spectacle Over Mile Long.
The National Service parade through the streets of Oxford yesterday afternoon, in support of the City's War Weapons Week, was the largest parade ever seen in Oxford, and it was watched by many thousands of people. *Oxford Mail*, Monday 2nd December 1940.

British warplanes photographed over Oxford during a flight in connection with the City's War Weapons Week. *Oxford Mail*, Saturday 7th December 1940.

Col. Chamberlayne inspecting the Oxford Home Guards in the University Parks yesterday morning. With him is Mr. G. Gosselin, who commands the Headington and Marston Company and behind is Capt. J.A. Douglas, the Battalion Commander of the Oxford City Home Gaurds. *Oxford Mail*, Monday 2nd December 1940.

Members of the ATS in the procession

Indian troops who took part in yesterday's National Service parade – the first time they had appeared in connection with a War Weapons Week event.

Members of the Home Guard in yesterday's big National Service parade through Oxford in connection with the city's War Weapons Week. *Oxford Mail*, Monday 2nd December 1940.

Oxford War Weapons Week. The £1,000,000 Passed – More to Come. Oxford War Weapons Week total has passed the new level of £1,000,000 for which the Mayor appealed. To-night the week ends and it is hoped that the total by then will have reached £1,250,000. *Oxford Mail*, Saturday 7th December 1940.

Over The Million Mark: The Indicator at Carfax showing that War Weapons Week investments had passed the million. *Oxford Mail*, Monday 9th December 1940.

[November] 1940

Dear Mummy and Daddy,

Thank you very much indeed for the torch; it is coming in very useful as the Jerries (d—. them) come over on their way to Coventry and Birmingham nearly every night.

Have they been over Stafford yet? (I've had no letters to tell me whether you have [been] bombed out or not.) The other night we had an 11 hour raid, but I missed little sleep.

I had my first trio the other week in 'Justorum animae' by Stanford.

Chapel services are now at 5.30 p.m. instead of 6.15.[52]

---

[52] In 1940 the clocks weren't put back at the end of summer (last Sunday in October), meaning Britain stayed one hour ahead of Greenwich Mean Time during the winter. In the spring of 1941 the clocks were still put forward an hour (last Sunday in March), meaning Britain was two hours ahead of GMT during the summer of 1941. The extra evening daylight gave people longer to get home before the blackout. This remained the case until 1947.

I'm sorry if this letter is late, but I started on Monday and finished today (Wednesday).

If you please can send a parcel, I would like some chocolate,[53] some chocolate biscuit fingers, and some 'Branston Pickle' (Crosse and Blackwells).

With the money that Granny sent me I bought a lovely naval book. I think the girls will like the other book, which is called 'Isle of Adventure' by A.S.K. Davis.

Your loving son, Shirley

P.S. Give my love to the girls and Spitfire.

Diana and Joan, the two evacuee girls from Ramsgate, together with a puppy (likely to be Spitfire) who were billeted with Michael's parents at 45 Rising Brook, Stafford in 1940.

---

[53] *The Lily*, the school magazine of December 1940 reported that 'Despite numerous air-raid warnings here at the School war still seems very remote. The greatest hardship that we have yet had to bear is a shortage of chocolate.'

Regular small air raids on the Midlands were conducted by the Germans during August through to early November 1940. This then escalated to major raids from mid-November onwards. A regular flight path for the Luftwaffe to the major Midlands towns was over Oxford, hence Michael's reference to the regular air-raid warnings during this time, but thankfully there were no raids on Oxford itself. Due to wartime censorship specific town names were often not mentioned in news reports, only bombing of a 'Midland town' was reported. However, the massive raid on Coventry on the night of Thursday 14th November and the subsequent devastation of the city and destruction of cathedral was reported in the *Oxford Mail* the next day.

Main headline: **COVENTRY HEAVILY ATTACKED. CASUALTIES MAY NUMBER 1,000. Cathedral Destroyed.** Germany launched the biggest night attacks yet made on this country during the hours between dusk last night and daybreak to-day. Left picture: **The End of a Raider:** Junkers bomber brought down near Blewbury. *Oxford Mail*, Friday 15th November 1940.

Main headline: **RAIDERS BOMB LONDON. Heavy Death Roll Feared In One Area**.
London suffered an exceptionally heavy raid last night. Two more hospitals were
among the buildings damaged. One A.R.P. worker said that for numbers of raiders
it was the worst night he had experienced.
Right picture: Members of the Oxford University O.T.C. including Cadets,
who are undergraduates under a War Office order. *Oxford Mail*,
Saturday 16th November 1940.

[Winter] 1940

Dear Mother and Father,

I am just writing a note to thank you very, very much for the stamps
and the sixpence. The brown stamp unused, as you sent it is worth
nearly 2/-.

Today it has been raining 'taxis and omnibuses' but now it is clearing up.

I've joined up with Turner and we're selling stamps. Already we have
got 1s/1d. You see, we divide the money equally.

I'm afraid I can't write any more as it is nearly teatime,

Yours, Shirley.

As for all towns and cities across Britain during the war, many of Oxford's metal railings and street furnishings were removed and used in tank and munitions manufacture. Many other, non-metal objects and statues were also removed for preservation or to minimise danger, such as the flagstones and Great War memorial of the front quad of Magdalen College, a site that Michael had become familiar with on his way to Chapel each day.

TRANSFORMATION OF THE MAGDALEN COLLEGE QUADRANGLE: To lesson danger from a bomb. *Oxford Mail*, Saturday 14th December 1940.

Oxford's famous Martyrs' Memorial presents an unfamiliar appearance. The railings which surrounded it have been removed to provide scrap iron for the country's war effort. *Oxford Mail*, Tuesday 2nd July 1940

If the street level appearance of Oxford was changing, Oxford University's sporting scene attempted to continue undeterred and crowds keen to have their mind taken off the war, at least for eighty minutes, flocked to watch the rugby at Iffley Road.

An Oxford University player brought down in Saturday's match at Iffley Road by one of Major R.V. Stanley's XV. Flight-Lieut. A.B. Rodger, Dean of Balliol, 'well known to Rugby fans' acted as a linesman. He is Dean of Balliol. *Oxford Mail*, Monday 25th November 1940.

Cambridge Win Rugby Match: Impressive play against Oxford. No official Oxford versus Cambridge Varsity Rugby match, traditionally staged at Twickenham since 1921, was played during the war, but a series of twelve unofficial games between the two sides were played in either city during the course of 1939-44. This article reports that for the postponed game of 7th December 1940 'There was quite a large attendance, which included some old Blues and many schoolboys. The ground looked in fine condition'. *Oxford Mail*, Saturday 7th December 1940.

As is still the case today, the facilities and outward tranquillity of Oxford and its colleges were utilised during the war as a place of retreat for many organisations during the war to hold conferences and meetings.

LONDON A.R.P. HEROES IN OXFORD. Stretcher Bearers Find Rest and Quiet at Magdalen College. This week Oxford has been entertaining a further number of London A.R.P. personnel in connection with the scheme which has been established for providing a brief holiday from the stress and strain of their duties. *Oxford Mail*, Saturday 14th December 1940.

In 1940 it was passed that wartime BA degrees from Oxford would be given after three terms of residence, followed by sitting simplified exam papers, as long as this was followed with War service. Later in the War, this changed to six terms of residence plus a six-week term in the summer holiday. Only those students that committed to the teaching profession were allowed to take three-year degrees. The restricted degrees didn't significantly change the appearance of Oxford with its familiar student chattels.

LECTURE TIME: A picture outside the Taylorian Institute, Oxford, which speaks for itself. *Oxford Mail*, Wednesday 14th October 1942.

OXFORD WAR-TIME BA DEGREE.
Not comparable to Cambridge, alleges
St Edmund Hall Head. *Oxford Mail*,
Wednesday 11th December 1940.

Spring (Hilary) Term 1941

The highlight of Michael's Spring term of 1941 was undoubtedly the Walter Parratt commemoration service held in the Magdalen College Chapel on 10th February 1941. Michael's love of choral music and the esteem to which he held the great and good of British music gathered

for the service that day was to stay with him and influence him for the rest of his life.

Michael's service programme for the Walter Parratt commemoration in Magdalen College Chapel, 10th February 1941, complete with autographs of the great and good of British choral music.

Monday 10th February 1941

Dear Mummy and Daddy,

I'm sorry that this letter is being written later than usual, but I was so excited yesterday that I really couldn't.

The reason I was so excited yesterday was that today there was a great commemoration service in the College Chapel for Sir Walter Parratt,[54] and the choir of St George's Chapel, Windsor, came over to sing with our choir.

Of course, I collected some <u>super</u> autographs; they included Dr Ernest Bullock, of Westminster Abbey; Dr Harris of Windsor; Sir Hugh Allen; Dr H. G. Ley; Dr Sydney Nicholson, and many others including Sir Walter Parratt's son, Geoffrey Parratt. We sang several Anthems – they were: 'Beati quorum via' by C.V. Stanford; 'The face of death' by W. Parratt; 'All go unto one place' by S.S. Wesley; and 'Blest pair of Sirens' by C.H.H. Parry. Sir Hugh Allen gave an address on the life of Sir Walter Parratt, which was very interesting.

Last night, for the first time, I went up into the organ-loft for the organ voluntary; that was also very good.

Your loving son, Shirley.

P.S. I will send you my programme of the commem. service during the week. It is simply <u>covered</u> with autographs.

Summer (Trinity) Term 1941

On the morning of Thursday 1st May *The Oxford Times* reported that 'a large crowd which included both young and old residents and evacuees, gathered at six o'clock in the morning for the traditional May Morning ceremony from the summit of Magdalen College Tower.' It went on to explain that 'It is customary, after the hymn, for the bells to peal, but that pleasant sequence this year, of course, was unheard, owing to the war-time ban on the ringing of church bells'.

---

[54] Walter Parratt (b.1841, d.1924) was organist at Magdalen College from 1872 until 1882, when he became organist of St George's Chapel, Windsor Castle. He became Heather Professor of Music at Oxford University in 1908, taking over from Hubert Parry.

May Morning at Oxford. The Cherwell was crowded with punts at 6am this morning when the choirboys sang from Magdalen College Tower.

The scene at Magdalen Bridge this morning at 6am.

Oxford Mail, Thursday 1st May 1941.

Sunday 4th May [1941]

Dear Mummy and Daddy,

In response to one of your questions in the letter (received yesterday), I don't think that my grub store needs replenishing just yet. I have eaten nearly all my chocolate, but there is still plenty more tuck of other sorts.

I expect you are waiting for an account of May Day[55], well here it is:- We got up at 5.10a.m. and were on the tower by 5.45. While we were singing a recording was taken; also a Movie-camera film was taken.* It will form part of a 'Paramount' film on old-world England or something daft, so look out for it! Also some photos have been taken of us crossing Magdalen Bridge after a practice. These will

[55] At this time the school always had an official holiday on 1st May. This school tradition continued until just after the Early May Bank Holiday (first Monday in May), which had been observed in Scotland since 1871, was introduced to the rest of the United Kingdom in 1978.

appear in the paper 'Illustrated' in about a fortnight. So will you please buy that copy?

Your loving son, Shirley

* a close-up was taken of me!

Sunday [Summer 1941]

Dear Mummy and Daddy,

Here is my weekly letter with as much information I can think of.

The other day I received a letter from Pilot-Officer Mckie, (who is still stationed at Torquay), and I have also received two letters from Jean [Spinks].

I'm afraid that if you want to give Taylor the chocolate you will have to wait for their train on Friday, as they are travelling on that day to avoid the crowded Saturday trains.

The mumps has been taking a fairly heavy toll of people – including both the Lyndons, the biggest one having it very badly.[56]

I have got my tuck-box tidied up, and in it is a lemon[57], which might be bad when it gets home, but you can cut the rotten part out – and there you are!

With best wishes from Shirley xxx

Despite many setbacks in the first few years of the war, small British victories like the sinking of Bismarck, see *Oxford Mail* headlines below, were clung to by the school boys and Michael, remembering fondly his care free school days, pointed out 'I think school boys are

---

[56] Many MCS cricket fixtures versus other schools during the summer of 1941 had to be cancelled due to the mumps outbreak at the school. Nationally, 1941 is considered to have been the greatest mumps epidemic, when approximately 250 cases were reported for every 100,000 people.

[57] Lemons, like bananas, all but disappeared from Britain for the entire war. They did not appear on the list of foods limited by rationing as they were so rare. It is therefore understandable why Michael was wanting to share his rare treat with his parents. Occasionally fresh oranges got through to Britain from America but children and pregnant women were invariably given priority for these by greengrocers.

always very optimistic. We were always winning; we were overjoyed when the Russians came in [to the war].[58] We kept great maps in our studies and our school atlases were covered in great arrows showing where our brave Russian allies were advancing. Our arrows were always grossly over optimistic, in the days of the invasion of Prussia there were huge arrows pointing at Berlin, but we soon realised that things weren't going awfully well for Marshal Budyonny and his gallant men who were surrendering in their hundreds and thousands believing that they had been liberated.' Michael is referring here to Semyon Budyonny, the Commander-in-Chief of the Soviet army facing the German invasion of the Ukraine, part of Germany's Operation Barbarossa. Operating under strict orders from Stalin to not retreat under any circumstances, Budyonny's forces were eventually surrounded during the Battle of Uman and the Battle of Kiev resulting in 1.5 million Soviet men being killed or taken prisoner. It is considered to be the largest encirclements in military history.

Main headline: **BISMARCK SUNK - OFFICIAL. Germans Lose Biggest Battleship.**
HOOD SPEEDILY AVENGED. The news of this victorious end to one of the most exciting naval chases in history was given to the world to-day by Mr. Churchill, and the British Prime Minister's announcement was followed shortly by an Admiralty communique stating: - 'The German battleship Bismarck has been sunk by our naval forces. Details of the operation will be announced as soon as possible.'
Picture, centre: **Oxford Home Guards Parade**: Brig-Gen McMullen inspecting the local Home Guard, who paraded in Oxford University Parks.
Oxford Mail, Tuesday 27th May 1941.

---

[58] On the 22nd June 1941, Germany launched an attack, 'Operation Barbarossa', on the Soviet Union, effectively moving the Soviet Union onto the Allies side in the war against Germany and Italy.

Despite the number of air raids on British cities drastically diminishing from March 1941 onwards, the threat of Oxford being bombed was still considered significant enough for new shelters to be constructed.

A new style surface shelter outside St. John's College, Oxford. *Oxford Mail*, Friday 23rd May 1941.

The surface shelter which is being erected in Alma Place, Oxford. Residents have protested. *Oxford Mail*, Wednesday 7th May 1941.

Keeping up appearances of the strength of homeland defence and resolve was crucial for public moral throughout the war, especially during the early years. Parades in Oxford, like the one seen below in the University Parks, were common place and typical of those seen throughout the country.

A general view of the Oxford Home Guard on parade in the University Parks. *Oxford Mail*, Tuesday 27th May 1941.

Autumn 1941 – Summer 1942

Ovaltine, Shakespeare and Pearl Harbour

In September 1941 Michael embarked upon his third year at MCS. He turned twelve on the 16th of the month and, as he rejoices in his first letter of the new term, he has been given the responsibility of being a soloist for the Magdalen Choir. At this point he was fast gaining the confidence that boarding away from home can sometimes help to foster. Luckily his voice broke much later than for many choristers and he was able to remain a chorister for longer than he had expected. This ultimately gave him the opportunity to achieve the position of Head Chorister after a further three years, a role of which he was immensely proud, following in his father and grandfathers footsteps.

Autumn (Michaelmas) Term 1941

Sunday [Autumn 1941]

Dear Mummy and Daddy,

Great news this week! – I am proud to state that I am now a soloist of Magdalen College Chapel, Oxford. During this last week I've had three solos, and on Thursday I'm singing [the] higher part in a duet.

TO-day Taylor and I are going to tea at Dr Wiggin's [Wiggins'], as the doctor told me to 'bring a pal if he wants to come'.

Yesterday the first XV played a losing match with King's School, Worcester.[59]

Talking about business; my Maths is letting me down so much that the house-master has offered me extra maths tuition with Lyndon Minor, who is also very poor at maths. Please tell me as quickly as you can.

Your loving son, Shirley

V ●●—

---

[59] Played at MCS, the result of the game was a loss for MCS 5-14.

P.S. The drawing is almost finished!

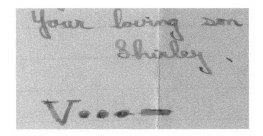

This and many other of Michael's letters were finished with a letter V and •••— the Morse code for V, presumably for Victory.

Wednesday [Winter 1941]

Dear Mummy and Daddy,

I'm ever so sorry that my letter hasn't been written before to-day as on Sunday I went out with a society known as the 'Antiquarians'. It is quite interesting, as we explore churches etc.

Terrific news, by gum! ① The choristers are staying on for Xmas! ② I was fourth in form! ③ I have been taken out to tea by a master of the school.

I have just been up to the City Library with Taylor – we are both members. Of course, it is free, and there are good books there in the children's department.

About this extra week.[60] I have met Mr. Blackwell[61], and he says that I will be able to spend part of the time at his house, 7 miles out of Oxford, if possible! Also, the science master will let us 'muck about' in the 'Chemy-lab.' – while he's there, of course!

---

[60] Choristers stayed on at school an extra week, compared to all other boys, in the run up to Christmas so they could partake in the College services and celebrations.

[61] Basil Blackwell was a former MCS pupil (1901-07) who overlapped with Michael's father by one term. Despite becoming head of Blackwell's family bookshop and publishing business he kept a keen interest in his old school, working as a rowing coach in his spare time until the 1920s and becoming heavily involved with the Old Boy's Club. He later became Chairman on the School's Board of Governors and eventually a Benefactor to the School.

No more news so goodbye from your loving son, Shirley

V ••• —

*Michael included a picture of boot treading on a
swastika at the end of this letter*

Michael did more than explore churches and recalled that in their 'free-time' on Sunday afternoons they would venture around the city 'discovering the roofs of most of the college chapels and frequently invading their hallowed organ lofts, switching on the electricity to work the bellows, and thundering away on the organs until chased off the premises by their infuriated but lawful custodians'. Through these exploits together with his Sunday afternoon exploration of sites like the Wittenham Clumps and places such as the University Museum, Ashmolean Museums and the New Theatre, Michael admitted 'quite unwittingly, we were educating ourselves'.

Sunday [Winter 1941]

My Dear Mummy and Daddy,

Thank you ever so much for the parcel – I forgot to thank you in the other letter, which I'm afraid was very late!

As we are staying on for Xmas (it is almost settled now) we shall either return on Christmas day or Boxing day. Nobody appears to know what's going to happen.

In answer to another question – what I would like for Xmas:-

① That book about ships that you promised me last 'vac'.

② 'How to draw planes' (if you ask the lady at the counter, ask for 'How to draw planes' by a man called Wooton.[62]

③ A bicycle lamp (and or) a torch.

④ * A bag for my bike (to fit on the saddle).

⑤ A decent bell or horn.

If that is too much, I don't mind if you exclude the bag.

Please thank Mrs Baron very much indeed for the naval button; I am very pleased with it, as I wear it as a button-hole.

Some R.A.M.C. men are down by first bridge now with a motor pump and a hose-pipe. I've just been down to have a look.

Your loving son, Shirley

---

[62] Frank A.A. Wooton's book went on to be a best-seller. In 1939, after volunteering for the RAF he was invited to accept a special duty commission as official war artist to the R.A.F. and Royal Canadian Air Force.

More doodling at the end of this letter, with Michael caricaturing his father's friend and Police colleague, Eric Brereton.

At the end of the Autumn term, the Choristers had to stay on in Oxford to sing services in the College Chapel during Christmas week. The choristers enjoyed the extra duty as they had the run of School House and the days were theirs when not in the practice room. By ancient custom the choristers were required to perform in the College hall for the Fellows and their guests on Christmas Eve, then afterwards they were rewarded at the Fellows' party with a feast in front of a huge Christmas tree and presents handed out by Oxford celebrities such as C.S. Lewis. They were also allowed to drink 'College Cup', a drink the boys imagined was a highly alcoholic brew and one that they thought would produce speedy inebriation. Choristers were then free to travel home for their holiday on either Christmas Day or Boxing Day.

[December 1941]

Dear Mummy and Daddy,

The first thing to be dealt with today in my letter is travelling on Boxing day. If I go by L.M.S. as usual, I will only have one boy with me until Bletchley, whereas if I go by G.W.R. I will have two people with me until

Wolverhampton. They are Matron and Metcalfe; I'm not quite sure if Matron will travel on Boxing day, but there is a chance that she will.

On Friday I sang a quartet in 'Why rage fiercely the heathen' by Mendellsohn [sp. Mendelssohn], and yesterday I partook in a duet in Stainer in A.

During the last week of this term the Choral Society is going to sing most of the 'Messiah', and I am doing as a solo 'He shall feed his flock', or rather, the treble bit, 'Come unto him'.[63]

As Christmas is near, our study (Top Little) has individually subscribed for decorations, and everything looks very bright with mistletoe, holly, ivy etc.

This next week brings exams, - I think that I'll be fairly high, as I've been swotting up like billy – ho!

As a final plea; may I please have some more Ovaltine or Bourn-vita as I have just run out. A quarter-of-pound will do.

Please give my best wishes to 'Twinks' and Mrs Barron – I'm looking [forward] to seeing them very much indeed.

Your loving son, Shirley.

On 7th December 1941 Japan launched air attacks on US bases at Pearl Harbour, Guam and Wake Island and naval bombardments of Midway Island, bringing the United States into the war against Japan, and ultimately, on 11th December 1941, against Germany and Italy. Later, in 1942 and 1943, Michael recalled that American soldiers and especially 'the most attractive American nursing sisters' (due to nearby US military hospital(s) preparing for the eventual invasion of Europe) becoming a common sight on the streets of Oxford as the US built up its military presence in Britain, 'They gave us chewing gum and sweets. They were fascinated by seeing small boys walking

---

[63] The performance of the Messiah took place in the School Chapel on Thursday 18th December 1941.

around the streets in mortar boards, gowns and Eton collars. .... they thought it was very cute and we were always posing for photographs.'

December 1941 was a desperately depressing time for the British population, when they were greeted with news of the start of the Japanese campaigns, Michael remembers his own reaction, '[HMS] Prince of Wales and Repulse, lost, they can't be, they're British, they're Royal Navy!'.[64] Michael explained the feeling and painted a picture of the propaganda at the time, 'Everybody was in a state of deep shock. We had been told the Japanese couldn't fly aeroplanes because their eyesight was bad. That their aeroplanes anyway were made from bamboo and wooden frames with canvas and were no match for our Bruster Buffalos and Vickers Vildebeests. And, anyway the guns of Singapore made it impregnable, and the collapse of the Anglo-Indian army in Malaya was regarded with horror. I remember gloomily filling in the map in my atlas, shading in the Japanese [territory gains] as the 'Rising Sun' moved south.'

Spring (Hilary) Term 1942

During the war, The Ministry of Food produced many 'Food Fact' adverts to promote healthy and frugal eating habits. In Michael's letter of 11th March, below, he thanks his mother for the parcel of Household Milk. The controlled distribution of liquid milk had begun in November 1941[65] and to supplement this, from December, tins of dried skimmed milk powder, known as Household Milk, went on sale. Each small tin was said to equal four pints of liquid milk when water was added and, for most of the war, every family was allowed one tin a month. Barely drinkable by itself, it was considered significantly better than nothing in coffee or cocoa and just better than nothing in tea, but really came into its own in cooking. The

---

[64] The battleship HMS Prince of Wales and the battlecruiser HMS Repulse were sunk by land-based long-range torpedo bombers of the Imperial Japanese Navy on 10 December 1941, just north of Singapore, off the east coast of Malaya.
[65] The usual amount of liquid milk allowed per week was from 2 to 2½ pints per person/ration book.

Ministry of Food also created a second type of powdered milk called National Dried Milk, a dried 'full cream' milk powder aimed at feeding infants.

This advertisement (Food Facts N0. 131), which actually appeared in the *Oxford Mail* in January 1943, was typical of the many Food Fact adverts produced by The Ministry of Food during the war.

'when fresh milk is scarce, take up your full share of **Household Milk**. ... . You can use it with your fresh milk in tea or coffee or by itself in puddings or cakes. Remember, Household Milk has all the goodness of milk – except the fat.   Household Milk helps to build sturdy bodies and makes teeth and bones sound. ... pop that blue and silver tin into your shopping bag when there's a share out. It's nine penn'orth of nourishment you can't afford to miss.'

Wednesday [11th March 1942]

My dear Mummy and Daddy,

I am really ever so sorry that I haven't written until so late a time during the week, but all the same, I've got plenty of things to write about.

Firstly, I thank [you] very much for last week's parcel; the Household Milk is coming in very useful. Also, I'm very grateful to you for the P.O.

Now comes the big news! To-day, I went with a large party of M.C.S. boys – guess where-?!! We went to see 'The Merchant of Venice' at the New Theatre!!! We went in the 3/- pit stalls; (money on the bill). The acting company belonged to the 'Old Vic' theatre in London! I thought it was simply gorgeous!!

And to-morrow, the School Choral Society (of which I am a member), and the School Orchestra are giving a concert in the Town Hall! There will be a huge audience, as at all concerts there; I only wish you could be present!

Last week I was eleventh in form, which is really fairly good for me.

Well now I really must say good-bye, as it will soon be time for chapel.

Your loving son

Shirley

xxx

V •••—

Michael's quick sketch of what he thought should happen to Hitler and Tojo[66] appeared at the end of this letter.

P.S. We're putting up a lousy show against the Japs. They seem to be everywhere.

Glad to hear we've bombed Paris.

---

[66] Hideki Tojo was the Supreme Military Leader of Japan from 1936 until 1944. After the war he was arrested, tried and sentenced to death for war crimes. He was hanged in December 1948.

THE MERCHANT OF VENICE. *Oxford Mail*, Saturday 7th March 1942.

Soon after sending this letter Michael became ill with mumps and was not able to write any more letters for the rest of the term. At the end of term, still too ill and infectious to return to Stafford, Michael and another boy were packed off to the Oxford Isolation Hospital at The Slade, next to the Cowley Barracks, and only released when pronounced 'fit for public exposure'.

Summer (Trinity) Term 1942

Saturday 3rd May 1942

Dear Mummy and Daddy,

As you can guess, there is plenty of news this week to tell you.

As usual we sang on the tower on May day. After a college breakfast,[67] we, (I mean the choristers) went out on the river with the academical

---

[67] Each year after singing on May Day, the choristers were treated to a 'sumptuous breakfast in the Senior Common Room [of the College] under the benevolent gaze of the Fellows.'

clerks, one of whom fell into the river! In the afternoon, another chorister and I lay in our 'binge'[68] and drank 'Corona' fruit drinks. By the way, thank you very much indeed for the P.O. I'm not changing it yet, as I've still got over 5/- left.

Yesterday, I created my own record for cricket. I played wicket-keeper in the first innings, and actually managed to stump a boy out! When our side went in to bat I hit up 13 runs for the side, that being the highest score in the whole game. Also, I scored the winning hit!

Nothing else to say so goodbye, from Shirley

V•••—

P.S. Tell you my form order next week.

On the same day as the *Oxford Mail* reported on the massive advance by the Japanese army through Burma (beyond the town of Lashio, effectively cutting the Allies supply chain to China), a menacing account of a second air raid in a fortnight on Exeter was reported. The previous week the historic towns of Bath, Norwich and York were also attacked, leaving other historic towns concerned they would be next. Later referred to as the 'Baedeker raids', these attacks targeted British towns designated of great cultural interest in Baedeker Guide books in retaliation for the RAF bombing of the historic German cities Lubeck and Rostock.

Two ominous headlines: **JAPS PUSH 65 MILES BEYOND LASHIO** and **Another 'Reprisal' Raid on Exeter**.
Oxford Mail, Monday 4th May 1942.

---

[68] 'Binges' were dens set up in the summer on the banks of the Cherwell to which boys would carry rugs and cushions and spend their idle hours reading and consuming 'tuck'.

The bombing of the historic city of Canterbury at the end of May, then twice at the start of June and again in October 1942 sent a signal that no town or city could consider themselves safe. The expectation that Oxford would be bombed at some stage was real and thus any dereliction of duty by an ARP or Fire Watcher was punishable with a fine, as experienced by Mr Jesse Webb of Oxford who received a £5 fine for failing to perform fire watching duties.

First Fine for Fire-Watch Default. *Oxford Mail*, Friday 6th March 1942.

Sunday [24th May 1942]

Dear Mummy and Daddy,

Thank you ever so much for the parcel and the money; the maids-of-honour were simply delicious – the best you've ever made – I gave one of them to Coleman, who enjoyed it very much.

This afternoon, I'm going to the 'Sheldonian' to hear a performance of the 'Mass in B minor' by Bach. I won't have to pay anything, as the organist, Mr Webster, is taking about half a dozen choristers into the organ gallery, from whence a good view is to be obtained of the proceedings.

Dr Stewart is better now, and will start taking services again this week.[69]

---

[69] Sadly, Haldane Stewart was to die only a few weeks later on 14th June 1942. On the night of the College's annual open-air madrigal concert under the Founder's Tower in the main College quadrangle, Stewart fell downstairs and broke his neck. He was given the customary full musical funeral by the College and the funeral was attended by some of the nation's most distinguished musicians.

On Saturday members of Magdalen College are giving a performance of 'Midsummer night's dream' in the college grounds, and the choristers are going to be fairies! We shall have to sing a chorus out of Mendelssohn's setting of the play, and we'll be all dressed up in fairies clothes. All this will be in the evening, lasting until about nine o'clock.[70]

I hope that Gangipop has received my letter.

From your loving son, Shirley.

The Oxford Times, Friday 29th May 1942

The programme from the OUDS production of *A Midsummer Night's Dream*, 4-6th June 1942.

---

[70] *A Midsummer Night's Dream* was actually being performed by the College and the choristers the following week, from Thursday to Saturday 4th-6th of June.

Throughout the war, newspapers presented the latest updates of the war alongside the everyday goings-on of local life. The contrast between these 'different worlds' was never starker than those reported in the *Oxford Mail* on Thursday 4th June 1942, when the headlines were of the 'Commando Raid on France'[71] and 'Bremen Bombed ...', and below were the pictures and report of the tranquil and idyllic performance of A Midsummer Night's Dream in the Magdalen College Grove. Not mentioned in the newspaper at the time were the devastating reverses for the British Eighth Army, happening in North Africa during May and June of 1942, when 50,000 allied men were either killed, wounded or captured, including 35,000 prisoners taken at Tobruk on 21st June 1942.

Left: Elaine Brunner (Helena), Michael Landon (Demitrius), Sonia South (Hermia) and John Hodgson (Lysander) in the Oxford University Dramatic Society's production of *A Mid-summer Night's Dream*, which will be given in Magdalen College Grove, Oxford, tonight. Above: Miss Patricia Morris (Hippolyta) and Mr Ian Husband (Theseus). *Oxford Mail*, Thursday 4th June 1942.

---

[71] The British Commando raid on France on the night of 3rd June 1942 was one of fifty-seven commando raids to take place against Hitler's Atlantic Wall between 1940 and 1944. The raid on this specific night, 'Operation Bristle', targeted a German radar site at Plage-Ste-Cecile between Boulogne and Le Touquet.

Taking a leaf out of Sir Walter Raleigh's book, students of Magdalen College remained unfazed by the war only 200 miles away and continued with their bowls.

Gowned Bowlers at Oxford: Bowling is a favoured recreation of Magdalen College undergraduates. They play on the College lawns. *Oxford Mail*, Friday 5th June 1942.

Keeping to the routines of a school year were crucial for the prosperity of the generation growing up in and just after the war. Here, Patrick Lyndon, one of Michael's best friends at MCS wins the 100 yards race at the 1942 Sports Day on School Field.

P.B. Lyndon winning the 100 yards race at the Magdalen College School sports at Oxford on Saturday. *Oxford Mail*, Monday 22nd June 1942.

Meanwhile, outside the school boarding house, on The Plain, with its familiar sight of the Victoria Fountain, the 'Oxford Salutes Russia' procession takes place.

Oxford Salutes Russia. PROCESSION, RALLY IN PARKS, AND APPEAL. Postwomen, railway women and the trade unions were well represented at the procession in Oxford on ther first anniversary of the German attack on Russia.

| Troops and A.T.S. at the head of the 'Salute to Russia' procession in Oxford yesterday. | A detachment of British Red Cross nurses in the parade at Oxford yesterday in tribute to our Russian Allies. |

Oxford Mail, Monday 22nd June 1942

Oxford during the war was never short of opportunities for school children to see and explore climbing over tanks. In July 1942, the *Oxford Mail* reported on a British A9 Cruiser tank used to promote Oxford women for war work.

Representatives of the Ministry of Labour, Ministry of Supply and local factories engaged on a campaign for recruiting Oxford women for war work. *Oxford Mail*, Wednesday 8th July 1942

Autumn 1942 – Summer 1943

Bells, Operation Carfax and Wings for Victory

Autumn (Michaelmas) Term 1942

Michael's experience of boarding, especially of being a chorister boarder, reached a defining moment in the autumn term of his fourth year in Oxford. 'We behaved like animals in a pack, forming alliances and then turning viciously on each other. It happened to me in the Michaelmas term of 1942 when I fancied myself as a pack leader of junior choristers who then, led by Barry Lyndon and Ken Morley, rounded on me and gave me a half term of misery. It was very physical and I remember my mother bursting into tears when she saw me in the bath on my first night back after the 'extra week' at Christmas, when the choristers ran amok with little or no supervision from the Master and with Horace Elam gone off on hols. I returned to school in trepidation next term and it started again on the first night in the junior dorm. Quite by chance the feeble defensive punch I aimed at Barry Lyndon connected awesomely and laid him flat on his back. Peace was achieved on the instant and we remained friends thereafter. We never seemed to bear long lasting grudges after these shifts of power; I suppose it was one of life's lessons being taught, albeit rather savagely.'

Sunday [1942]

Dear Mummy and Daddy,

Here is my weekly letter, and this is me writing it!

This week, on Tuesday, I just missed seeing a bloke attempting to commit suicide. He first threw himself under a car, which, however, missed him. He then threw himself over the parapet of Magdalen Bridge into the river. He was eventually fished out, but not before he had thrown two of his rescuers into the water.

I arrived just in time to see him lying unconscious on the bank, surrounded by policemen etc.

It is grand to be back in harness (ie. choir duties), as Mr Taylor is a very nice gentleman. He is going to take the whole choir out to the 'flicks'[72] when a good film comes along.

I'm afraid I can't write any more, 'cos I've been invited to play 'Commandos'.

From your loving son, Shirley.

V

On **13th** June 1940 the order had been communicated, via the wireless, that church bells must not be rung except for air raids and in the event of invasion. The ban remained in place until the Government decided that Sunday ringing of Church Bells could be recommenced on Easter Sunday, April 25th, 1943. On 27th May 1943 the ban on ringing church bells was lifted altogether. During the three years ban the church bells of Oxford were heard only twice and only during this Michaelmas term of 1942, on Sunday 15th November when special permission was given to celebrate the reversal of allied fortunes in North Africa and the Allied victory at El Alamein and in December permission was given to ring the bells on Christmas Day.

JOY BELLS IN OXFORD ON SUNDAY. Times at Which They Will be Rung. The Oxford Society of Change Ringers acting on the suggestion of the Prime Minister, has made arrangements for the ringing of the following bells on Sunday morning.
Oxford Mail, Thursday 12th November 1942.

A group taken at Christ Church Cathedral of some of those who rang victory peals in Oxford yesterday.
Oxford Mail, Monday 16th November 1942

---

[72] The term 'flicks' was and still is an affectionate name for the cinema, referring to the flickering motion and noise the old projectors made as they projected the moving image.

23 DECEMBER, 1942

Civil Defence
Faringdon Ex

PLANS FOR OXFORD'S BELLS

OXFORD, together with the rest of the country, will hear the Christmas bells this year, permission having been given by the Ministry of Home Security for them to be rung at any period between 9 a.m. and noon on Christmas Day.

The Oxford Society of Change Ringers requests that all available ringers shall assemble in the Cathedral belfry at 9 a.m. so that they can be detailed to the various churches.

It is hoped that they will respond as well as they did when the bells were rung for the victory in Egypt.

PLANS FOR OXFORD'S BELLS. Oxford, together with the rest of the country, will hear the Christmas bells this year.
Oxford Mail, Wednesday 23rd December 1942

Spring (Hilary) Term 1943

At the beginning of 1943, despite the reduced likelihood of invasion or major air-raid, the Oxford Civil Defence and military authorities went ahead with plans for a large scale 'War Exercise' to test the city's readiness for a heavy air raid or invasion. On Friday 15th January the city's population was warned of the upcoming exercise, which would use both a Saturday and Sunday, but told the date would be announced at a later time. The upheaval the exercise was going to produce caused much concern for the local inhabitants and workers and much correspondence was sent to the *Oxford Mail* in the weeks running up to the 'Invasion' raising concerns about disruption to work and travel. Officially known as 'Exercise Carfax', the two-day exercise took place on Saturday and Sunday, 30th and 31st January 1943.

The exercise involved the discharge of explosions on the ground to simulate heavy bombing from the air, simulated gas attacks, demolitions and deposition of rubble to simulate blocked roads and building fires and other incidents were staged across the city. Anyone not involved in a civil defence role was asked to stay in their homes in accordance with the official 'Stand Firm' policy. On the Sunday a strong military attack was enacted, involving tanks, with the local Home Guard forming the main defence. Farmers in the countryside immediately surrounding Oxford had prior warning because of likely disturbance to livestock by large troop movements.

The simulated action was played out next to Michael's boarding house, by The Plain. The report in the *Oxford Mail* gives a flavour of 'Exercise Carfax', the invasion of Oxford, and the excitement and disruption it would have caused: *'As a result of heavy 'bombing' at the approaches to Magdalen Bridge many areas, including Cherwell Street, Union Street, Iffley Road, George Street, St Clement's, Alma Place, and Stockmore Street were presumed cut off or damaged, in some circumstances the roads being blocked.'* ... *'The river was crossed [by the enemy] in two places, just south of Magdalen Bridge and north of the Northern By-pass. At a later point the infantry outflanked the defenders of the bridge by cutting across the fields and through the allotments. Although the suburbs of the city were in the hands of the 'enemy' before mid-day they failed to reach the centre and were held at Magdalen Bridge. A few tanks and infantry, after getting as far as this, were wiped out by the Home Guard.'*

Lead up to the invasion of Oxford, 'Exercise Carfax'

How Oxford's Two Days Of War Exercise Will Affect Public.
Oxford Mail, Friday 15th January 1943.

Oxford's Invasion Exercise.

Oxford Mail, Friday 22nd January 1943.

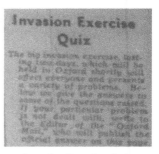

Invasion Exercise Quiz

Oxfords Citizens' Role In 'Invasion': Facts You
Should Know.

Oxford Mail, Friday 29th January 1943

'DIVE-BOMBING' OXFORD

Preparing for displaced persons

Above: The Mobile Assistance Unit which visited St Giles, Oxford, yesterday. These units are intended for the alleviation of air raid victims.

Right: The Mayor of Oxford (Counc. Mrs M. White) is interviewed by officials of the Mobile Assistance Board Unit, who treated her as a raid victim who had suffered material loss. She received an imaginary grant of £40 and a number of clothing coupons.

Oxford Mail, Saturday 23rd January 1943.

After the invasion of Oxford and the results of 'Exercise Carfax'

Main story: Although some 'enemy' tanks entered Oxford in the invasion exercise yesterday, when the sirens announced the conclusion of the exercise in the afternoon the flag was still flying at Carfax and the City was unconquered.

Picture right: Men and women firefighters in action during the exercise.

A low-flying bomber gives a realistic touch to the exercise.

An incident in Cornmarket during Oxford's big exercise when 'fire' started at the old Clarendon Hotel during the 'dive bombing attacks'.

The broken Cutteslowe wall at North Oxford, which was demolished by a defending tank to avoid capture during Sunday's exercise.

Members of the sectional engineer's department of the Post Office decontamination squad at work when 'gas' fell.

Capt.the Hon. Quintin Hogg, MP for Oxford City, one of the many official spectators of the military exercise in Oxford yesterday.

Oxford Mail, Monday 1st February 1943

Sunday [21st February 1943]

Dear Mummy and Daddy,

Thank you both very much for the money and the mince pies; I think that 'In which we serve' is starting at two cinemas in Oxford to-morrow. The mince pies were delicious, as several other people I gave one said!

Mrs Lovett's house, or rather her daughter's, is a lovely thatched cottage with a walnut tree on the front garden. They have got a funny Manx cat called 'Rumpy' as well as an ancient tabby. The house was built about 1599 and Cromwell is believed to have stayed there.

At this moment I am alone in the study, and a mouse is walking around on the floor by the radiator although I can't see it.

This morning I drove a smashing bargain with another boy; I lent him fourpence for half of his sweet ration! I am now planning on what to get with it. (I think I will let him off the fourpence!)

In the early hours of yesterday morning, the whole dorm were awakened by three tremendous bangs followed by four others. We learnt the next morning that it was a Commando exercise just outside the school-house.[73]

I don't know my form position yet, but I'll tell you next week.

I do hope that daddy's rheumatics are getting better; we have had no snow yet, and the trees are beginning to open out.

I have decided on the two people I would like to be taken out in a fortnight's time, they are Saunders and Metcalfe.

---

[73] Michael, in an interview in 1999, recalled 'we had huge exercises which swept through Oxford. They were invasion exercises and in 1943 there was one in which a battalion of Canadian troops defended Magdalen Bridge and curiously enough they dug lots of slit trenches and bunkers and there was lots of firing of blank ammunition night and day and to this very day it is still possible for the observant eye in the grounds of Magdalen College School to see traces of some of the trenches and dugouts they dug. We joyfully took them over when the exercise was over and converted them into dens in which we could smoke.

Well, goodbye for now, from Shirley

V ● ● ● —

I will be sending Polyfotos as soon as possible.

Michael's sketch of the old cottage at Appleton, near Abingdon, 1944

In an attempt to save fuel, many bus companies converted some of their vehicles to operate on producer-gas. These buses towed a small trailer containing a gas tank. The gas was produced by drawing air through hot anthracite coal or coke which was then piped through to the specially modified engine. Performance was poor, the buses were generally restricted to the flatter routes and re-fuelling was necessary every 80 miles or so. Most adapted buses were converted back to conventional operation well before the end of the war.

Oxford's first producer-gas driven bus photographed in service in Cowley Road.
Oxford Mail, Monday 15th February 1943.

Saturday [27th February 1943]

Dear Mummy and Daddy,

I have seen 'In which we serve',[74] and it was the best acted film I have ever seen. It was very sad at the end when Captain Kinross said goodbye to the survivors of his ship, and I blubbed; Mummy knows I haven't blubbed since that first time (!) at the pictures (touch wood), so it just goes to show what it was like!

---

[74] 'In Which We Serve' was written, directed and starred in by Noël Coward. This classic British wartime film received the full backing of the Ministry of Information, who facilitated the release of military personnel to take part in the film.

Gosh, I am jolly excited at seeing Mummy a week to-day; I am planning out what to do already. If it is wet on the Sunday I suggest that we go to a concert in the Town Hall; it is complete performance of the 'Messiah' with Eric Greene and Isobel Baillie, so it ought to be pretty good.[75]

I <u>might</u> be able to give you a solo on Saturday night, but I'm not quite sure yet.

On Tuesday I started an allotment with two other boys, so if you would care to bring some carrot seeds with you, I would be very pleased. Also, could you bring what's left of my model 'Rata',[76] I think it's in one of the junk drawers in my bedroom.

I will give Mummy the Polyfotos when she arrives. I will meet her at the Eastgate[77] if I am told the time.

From your loving son, Shirley.

---

[75] Eric Greene (b.1903, d.1966) was one of England's foremost oratorio tenors. During the Second World War, he was appointed organiser of the C.E.M.A. (Council for the Encouragement of Music and Arts) in Devon and Cornwall where for six months he arranged and took part in over six hundred factory concerts. Dame Isobel Baillie, DBE (b.1895, d.1983) was regarded as one of the 20th century's great oratorio sopranos.

[76] The 'Rata' was one nickname for the stubby looking Polikarpov I-16 fighter plane, a Soviet fighter aircraft of revolutionary design, being the world's first low-wing cantilever monoplane fighter with retractable landing gear. A must-have model for any boy of the era.

[77] The Eastgate Hotel, Oxford is located just a quarter of a mile from School House, near to the Ruskin School of Drawing and Fine Art and the Examination Schools on the High Street and the corner of Merton Street. Interestingly it is believed that the hotel is connected to Magdalen College by one of the many ancient tunnels that run under the city.

'Messiah' Performed At
Oxford. Oxford Mail,
Monday 8th March 1943

IN WHICH WE SERVE. Oxford Mail, Friday 19th
February 1943

IN WHICH WE SERVE.
Oxford Mail, Saturday
20th February 1943

Oxford had a Polyfoto studio on the High Street, at Webbers (9-15 High St). After their sitting, customers were sent a proof sheet of 48 poses, from which they could choose to order enlargements, booklets or cards of the best pose. Polyfoto had its heyday during the Second World War when Polyfoto cards were given as parting presents.

Polyfotos of Michael Hickey, aged 13.

Sunday [21 March 1943]

Dear Mummy and Daddy,

Yesterday I had the fortune to meet Captain Hazeler [Haseler], who said he was at Magdalen with you; he gave me 2/6, and told me that he is writing to you. He is in Oxford at present, but I don't know his address.

I had a super time at the Clapperton's last Sunday – I went into the mill, and sat in the garden with a pair of binoculars watching planes, after which I had tea consisting of a fried egg, fried bacon, sausage, fried spuds, and fried bread.

On Friday, I went to another party, and gave my host a bar of chocolate.

We stop services on Thursday (whoopee!) and only another ten days …… !!!!

Some fool of a boy has poured whitewash down the mouse hole, so I can't see my pen coming out in its true colours.

Owing to a collapse of maths, I was 21st in the form last week, but my marks this week are pretty high.

I was very sorry to hear of Barry Anderson's death.[78] I suppose he must have been wounded previous to his capture.

From your loving son, Shirley.

V ••• —

<hr>

Sunday night [1943]

Dear Mummy and Daddy,

This letter will, I'm afraid, be unavoidably late, as to-day, I have had no time to sit down and write.

I have just come back from the singing in the cloisters, which was very good indeed. Leslie Woodgate, the man in charge of the B.B.C. chorus was there, and he told Mr Taylor that it was very good. Ex-choristers all said that it was better than any other choristers singing we have ever done. We certainly all enjoyed singing in it.

This morning, we were a long time with last-minute rehearsing etc. and this afternoon, I went out with Saunders to tea with Canon Bisdee, and I had my first chocolate éclair for donkey's years.

[78] Barrie Sherwill Norman Anderson, a Trooper with the Royal Armoured Corps and No.1 Commando, and a Hickey family friend from Stafford, died in Italy on 12 January 1943, age 24.

Last Wednesday night, there being no chapel, I went with Edwards to hear the London Philharmonic Orchestra with Eileen Joyce[79] (piano). I think it is the best concert I have ever been to as regards performance and programme, and the Grieg Piano concerto was terrific. In the interval, I partook of some excellent cider, which made me sick during the night (mainly because of the amount of chocolate, toffee, etc. I had consumed during the performance.[)]

Very little else to say, except that I have got two mouse-traps, and have caught two mice since Saturday, much to the delight of the study!

From Shirley

Michael's sketch of a mouse at the end of this Sunday night letter.

Summer (Trinity) Term 1943

Friday [30th April 1943]

Dear Mummy and Daddy,

I'm sorry that I haven't written earlier in the week, as everything is still in confusion. My luggage arrived this afternoon, and I have got the film put in my camera. I am very excited about to-morrow; the singing starts at seven o'clock, so it might be broadcast (!)

---

[79] Eileen Alannah Joyce (1908-91) was a famous Australian pianist whose recordings made her popular internationally in the 1930s and 1940s and particularly during the Second World War.

I will tell you all the news on Sunday, when all the ferment will have died down.

Well, my time is almost up, but I will tell you that I was punctual on Tuesday, and that I got a seat after Bletchley.

From your loving son, Shirley

V •••—

Michael's sketch of Magdalen Tower, proclaiming 'THEY ARE GOING TO RING THE BELLS!' at the end of this Friday letter.

In April 1943 Winston Churchill announced to the House of Commons that the ban on Sunday service and special occasion church bell ringing would be lifted from Easter Sunday, April 25th 1943. Michael's excitement at the thought of the bells being rung for May Morning is evident from his sketch and exclamation in his letter of Friday 30th April 1943. A month later, on 27th May the ban on ringing church bells was lifted altogether. The threat of invasion and the number and size of air raids experienced by Britain in 1942 and 1943 had significantly diminished, so much so that the reservation of the bells for an early warning system was no longer required.

English Folk Dance Society in Cowley Place, outside Magdalen College School.

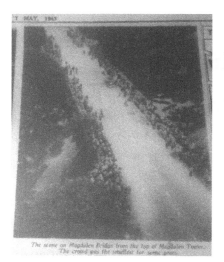

The scene on Magdalen Bridge from the top of Magdalen Tower. The crowd was the smallest for some years.

The choir singing the Latin Eucharist hymn, 'Te Deum Patrem Colimus' at the top of the Tower.

Oxford Mail, Saturday 1st May 1943.

The third anniversary of the Oxford Home Guard was celebrated Sunday 16th May, with a march past on South Parks Road.

Oxford people turned out in large numbers to watch the march-past of the Oxford Home Guard at the saluting base yesterday. A scene from the roof of Rhodes House. *Oxford Mail*, Monday 17ᵗʰ May 1943

To help raise money to purchase more bombers, national fund-raising events were held across Britain during the summer of 1943. The Oxford 'Wings For Victory Week' was held between 29ᵗʰ May – 5ᵗʰ June and included hands on exhibits for children and of course an obligatory military procession.

Main headline: **Programme of Oxford Wings for Victory Week 29 May – 5 June.**
Picture: **UNIVERSITY PARKS CRICKET PRACTICE** – A scene at the nets in the University Parks, Oxford, yesterday. *Oxford Mail*, Thursday 13ᵗʰ May 1943

The W.A.A.F.s made a smart turn-out in the Oxford Wings for Victory procession yesterday. *Oxford Mail*, Monday 17ᵗʰ May 1943

Sunday [6th June 1943]

Sunday

Dear Mummy and Daddy,

Well 'Wings for Victory' is over, and I enjoyed it very much. Last Saturday I went to an R.A.F. Exhibition and amongst other things looked inside the cockpit of a 'Tiger Moth' trainer, and dropped dummy bombs out of the practice bombing apparatus, which was great fun! Then I went to see two fighters, which were drawn up at the bus terminus. On Thursday I went to a 'Grand Féte' staged by the A.R.P. Dump near the school-buildings. I had sandwiches, jelly and a pony ride!

Something very unusual occurred in the early hours yesterday morning; the sirens went, and shortly afterwards the Oxford anti-aircraft guns went off with a terrific racket; we did not get up, but just lay in our beds watching the bangs and flashes. I believe they were firing at some Jerries coming over Boar's Hill. It was my first experience of anything like that, and at first I was a little windy, but the other boys were grand and didn't seem to mind a bit, so I soon lost all fright and soon went to sleep while the guns were still firing.

When I finish this letter I am going out to Mrs Lovett. She lives fairly near Abingdon Aerodrome, and must have heard a lot of shooting.

Last week something unpleasant occurred in form; someone (no-one knows who) stole the book with the marks in, and altered most of them, so that I came 23rd. Several other boys were down at the bottom of the form as well, owing to the dishonesty of this one person, who has not owned up.

Could you possibly send me a parcel, as all the grub I brought back to school was eaten up years ago.

Thank you very much for the money. I gave 6/- to 'Wings for Victory' and spent the rest on myself. I also got a very interesting book called 'Combined Operations 1940-42'. It only cost a bob[80] and is worth every penny of it.

---

[80] Bob, the slang term for a shilling coin.

Mr Shepperd sends his best to you, and hopes to meet you at Commem.[81]

Oh, by the way, I have looked it up on the College war memorial that B.H. Carter was the one killed in the Great War.[82] He was in the R.A.F.

It was very sad about Aunty B. but, as Mummy said in her letter, she had been in great pain and she is now where pain hurts no more.[83]

Well, since I am exhausted after the effort of writing this letter, I will now close down.

From your loving son.

Shirley

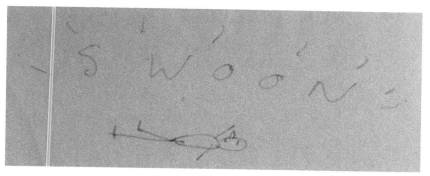

Michael's expression of exhaustion after writing this long letter

---

[81] Commem is the annual commemoration service held in honour of the benefactors of the school. Michael's parents rarely visited him during term time due to distance, lack of a family car and of finance, but always managed to get to Oxford for Commem. Such was Brian Hickey's love of the school and recognition of the importance of its Commem service that in 1927 he and Eveline spent their honeymoon in Oxford to go to the service and for Brian to play in the traditional Old Boys' cricket match and to attend the Old Boys' dinner.

[82] Bernard R.H. Carter, a contemporary of Michael's father, attended MCS from 1908-12 and was a chorister at the same time as his two older brothers Brian and George. Bernard, flying for the RFC, was killed when his plane crashed at Anglesey in November 1917.

[83] It is not known who this Aunty B was.

The 'Keep calm and carry on' attitude of the time was highlighted at the start of June 1943 when the main stand at the Oxford Stadium[84], home to the city's greyhound and speedway track, burnt down. The next day greyhound racing took place as normal with the main race of the meet being in aid of the Wings for Victory week. The Mayor of Oxford (Counc. Mrs White) presented the trophy.

Fire Disaster At Oxford Stadium. *Oxford Mail*, Friday 4th June 1943.

---

[84] The Oxford Stadium on Sandy Lane, Cowley, was built in 1938 and held motorcycle speedway until 2008 and greyhound racing until its closure in 2012.

Autumn 1943 – Summer 1944

*Head Chorister, Salute
the Soldier and D-Day*

Autumn (Michaelmas) Term 1943

Military activity in the form of residence of military schools within colleges, armed forces conferences, parades or ceremonies and even military exercises were as much, if not more, of a common feature of Oxford life during the war than most British towns or cities. The opportunity of the reduced student body to take part in military life whilst at university also gave Oxford the appearance of increased militarisation. Michael also recalled how more and more college space was taken up by various Whitehall departments and ministries, with senior officers of all three services routinely seen in Magdalen College. These uniformed servicemen were duly saluted by the choristers by removal of their mortarboards as they were 'capped'[85] by the officers in what became a customary salutation.

Vice-Admiral J.G.P. Vivian (Admiral Commanding Reserves) inspecting the Oxford University Naval Division at the passing-out ceremony at their headquarters in Christ Church Meadow yesterday. *Oxford Mail*, Wednesday 15th September 1943.

Air Chief Marshal Sir Charles Burnett inspecting the Oxford University A.T.C. at their passing out parade yesterday. *Oxford Mail*, Saturday 18th September 1943.

---

[85] Michael described 'capped' as the tipping of a military cap by way of recognition without a full salute.

Sunday 26th September 1943

Dear Mummy and Daddy,

In response for your request for news, I hereby write this letter. I had a very good journey all the way down both before and after Bletchley. The Polish paratroop officers were very nice indeed, as were the other people in the compartment. The little dog was a Yorkshire terrier, and was a super little thing. It kept jumping on and off our knees, the Poles, who were highly amused at its antics, gave it chocolate and took him for walks down the corridor. I was at Bletchley about a quarter of an hour before the Oxford train came in, and easily got a seat, although the train was crammed full by the time it reached Oxford. Everyone at school seemed very pleased to see me back, especially my ole' pals.

Our form order has not come out yet, but I'll most certainly tell you what place I was in next Sunday's letter.

Thank you very much for the wallet etc. I was beginning to think you had forgotten them.

Metcalfe has adopted a stray cat; it is a lovely tortoiseshell thing, and is comfortably at home on the Spit. Metcalfe has not imprisoned it, and it is free to go where it likes. The other night we saw it kill a vole; not a pleasant sight, but of course, it is nature.

Have you remembered to bring my bean in if the weather is cold? I am very pleased with its progress as reported in your letter.

There is very little else to say, except that the weather, though rather cold, is very sunny. How far is Aylesbury from Oxford? I expect that, if you go to Granny and Grandpa, you will be able to come and see me!

As far as I can make out, I am not entitled to any extra coupons, as I am 3 months too old, but I'll do my best.

From you loving son, Shirley.

V ••• —

Sunday [3rd October 1943]

Dear Mummy and Daddy,

I have some great news for you this week; last week, I was seventh in the form! I don't know my position this week yet, but I hope that it will be just as high.[86]

Could you possibly send me my stamps? I would like to swap some of them with Lyndon who has also brought his stamps to school.

I have bought some tin soldiers off other boys at school for a penny, twopence, or threepence, and have now quite an efficient little army.

Thank you very much for a lovely tart; it had fallen to pieces a bit, but it was lovely all the same.

I made enquiries, but I was told that I am not entitled to any extra coupons; my size was allright, but I was too old, the age being 13.9 (Chiz!)

Mrs Davis went into hospital for an operation on Thursday, and is now on the way to recovery.

A member of the 1st XV dislocated his knee cap in a rugger practice on Monday.

Yesterday the 1st XV licked Southfield all over the place, and won a match about 43-0 or something like that.

I am now having extra maths twice a week with the housemaster.

Would Daddy like to write to Mr Crusher,[87] the chaplain, saying that I'm to be confirmed? I have already told him that, but you had better confirm that personally.

---

[86] Michael's prediction for his place, or order of achievement in the Form of 24 boys was slightly optimistic. His Half-Term Report card for Michaelmas 1943 records that after being 7th in week 1, he slipped to 14th in week 2, eventually slumping to 24th place in week 6. Report cards in this era certainly didn't hide the truth.

[87] Michael was referring to the 'High Church persuasion' school chaplain, Rev E.W.H. 'Herbie' Crusha, who had been preparing him for Confirmation. When Michael's father, who had been brought up in a more conservative Anglican tradition, heard that

I had better close now,

With love from your loving son, Shirley.

V • • • —

P.S. I'm going for a walk with Saunders this afternoon; we are going to explore Port Meadow.

Despite the militarisation of the city, the cultural life of Oxford continued and Michael took continued to take advantage of the concerts, theatre and cinema that was on offer.

Sunday [24th October 1943]

Dear Mummy and Daddy,

Well, it is Sunday once more, and as I sit down to write this letter, I am thinking of what to say, as there is so much to put in such a little space.

It is a treat having Gangipop in Chapel on Wednesday, but he did not arrive till 4.30, by which time I was getting impatient, as I had been waiting at the gates all afternoon. We had a good anthem; - 'I was glad' by Parry, and I think he enjoyed it, although I missed him after the service.

This morning was filled up with a rehearsal at New College for the big concert. New Coll. and Christ Church have got dreadful choirs; New College sounds as if about four people are singing, and Christ Church yell at the tops of their voices and can't sing softly when required. I think that our choir is far better trained than theirs.

Apart from 'In Exitu' we aren't doing anything really thrilling.

Crusha intended to take confessions of all the candidates before the ceremony and that Michael had been chosen as the Bishop's acolyte, wrote a furious letter to the Master, Mr Davis, forbidding this. Michael was subsequently confirmed by the Suffragan Bishop of Dorchester the following year, in 1944.

Leon Goos[s]ens, the famous oboesist, is playing something or another, and the whole town is wildly excited at the idea of such a concert (!) (?)

Last Sunday evening Lord (or Earl) Harewood, came into chapel. He afterwards remarked that our choir was very good.

Last I walked, with Saunders, out to the little place called Elsfield;[88] it is a big hill, and from it there is a gorgeous view of Oxfordshire spread out underneath.

I really must go now, for I will probably miss the post.

I was 17 in form.

Thank you very much indeed for the parcel.

Yesterday I went to see 'My Learned Friend' with Will Hay and Claude Hulbert. It was very funny.

Could you please send me a spot of money.

From your loving son,

Shirley.

V ••• — xxxx

---

[88] Elsfield is 3.1 miles from MCS.

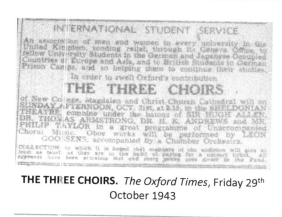

THE THREE CHOIRS. *The Oxford Times*, Friday 29th October 1943

GOOSENS IN SUITE BY MULGAN.
Oxford Mail, Monday 1st November 1943

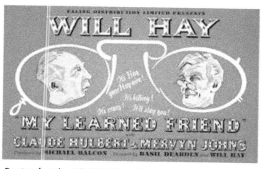

Poster for the 1943 British, black-and-white comedy farce, *My Learned Friend*.

Monday [1st November 1943]

Dear Mummy and Daddy,

I'm very sorry that I am writing late again; I couldn't write yesterday because of practice for the concert, and I couldn't write on Saturday because we had a practice all evening.

I had a great treat on Saturday: I went to the theatre! It was a very exciting play by Agatha Christie called 'Ten little Niggers', and had about 8 murders in it.

Yesterday the concert went off with a great success. Even when the Sheldonian was crammed full, the queue outside stretched down the Broad Street as far as Parker's book shop.[89]

On Friday I went to see Mr. Blackwell and he gave me some cake, and a list of the best books about tanks, ranging from 5/- to 15/-. I hereby enclose his list.

I got the letter from Jean, but, personally speaking, I didn't like the pictures very much. Her hair is not very nice now, and I hope she doesn't leave it like that.

The other night, I sang the solo in 'Justorum Animae', by Donkin, and Sir Hugh Allen and Dr Andrew's, the organist of New College, were in Chapel.

I'm afraid that I'll have to close down now with best wishes from your loving son, Shirley.

The Oxford Times, Friday
22nd October 1943

THREE CHOIRS CONCERT.
The Oxford Times, Friday
5th November 1943

---

[89] In 1964 Exeter College demolished the old Parker's bookshop at Nos. 26–27 Broad Street and built their Thomas Wood Building on the corner of the Broad Street and Turl Street. This is now the location of Blackwell's Art and Poster shop.

More 'special occasion' ringing of the bells in Oxford was heard in early November 1943 in honour of the new incoming Mayor of Oxford, Counc. H.C. Ingle, who was also the President of the Oxford Society.

Oxford Bellringers' Salute to Mayor
Oxford Mail, Thursday 11ᵗʰ November 1943.

Monday [15ᵗʰ November 1943]

Dear Mummy and Daddy,

This is a very important letter; in fact it is the most important I have written for a long time, as it contains some information which will possibly lead to me having a job of work in 2 year's time as a student of drama etc. at the B.B.C.

This is it. I found it this morning on the notice-board at school. It says, roughly: There are offered to boys of about 16½ who have passed School Certificate and are interested in the Arts, such as drama, etc. Applicants will be given six months training at something, and finish up at a salaried post on some B.B.C. staff. I will get more particulars and send them next week, and if you are willing, I will keep this in mind, as I am determined, really, to be either an actor or a B.B.C. announcer. Rather optimistic, you may think, but not if I back into it and work, work, work!

This evening, coming back from chapel, I saw a 'Whitley' bomber[90] caught in a searchlight beam; it looked just like a great pale green fish in a strong ray of light, and was very interesting to look at.

On Sunday I am going out to Boar's Hill, and am looking forward to it very much.

When Daddy next writes, will he please tell me what time he will arrive next Wednesday; tell him to come as early as possible, because there is the Old Boy's Rugger Match, which will start at about 2.30p.m.

On last Saturday the 1st XV beat Abingdon School 54-0. It was a very easy victory, and rather boring to watch.[91]

I do hope you will excuse the dreadful writing, as I am in a terrific hurry.

I went up to 13th in form this week, and am continuing to work hard.

Also, 'Je vais en bonne sante.' Which being translated, means: I am in good health.

From your loving son, Shirley

V ••• —

RUGBY. *The Oxford Times*, Friday 19th November 1943

Flight, 7th October 1937

---

[90] The Armstrong Whitworth Whitley was one of three British twin-engine, front line medium bomber types in service with the RAF at the outbreak of the Second World War (the others were the Vickers Wellington and the Handley Page Hampden).

[91] Attendance to watch 1st XV or 1st XI school matches was compulsory, with absence being rewarded by a beating.

Saturday [20th November 1943]

Dear Mummy and Daddy,

This letter is early because I am spending to-morrow out at Aunty Effie's, up Boar's Hill. I am looking forward to it very much, as she always puts out a terrific meal.

Also, I'm looking forward to Wednesday. Now here is something important. Mr Blackwell has written to me to say that if we meet him outside his shop at 12.45p.m., he will join us in lunch, as he would like to see you very much. I went to see him yesterday, and he filled me with seed. I think he is very nice, as he is always cracking jokes.

Matron has got me those extra 20 coupons, so we need not waste time on that account. If it is fairly warm, may I suggest that we watch part of the Old Boy's Rugger Match? Anyway, this is what I understand: (1) That you will meet me out of School. (i.e. near the telephone kiosk opposite the school house) at 12.30. We go and meet Mr. Blackwell outside his shop at 12.45. Then, we have the afternoon in front of us, after lunch.

I hope you are both well: it has been very cold here, but I keep well muffled up. Yesterday the river froze in places, but to-day it is not so cold, only misty.[92] To-night, the choir-boys of Leicester Cathedral came here to hear us sing, and I think they enjoyed it very much. Do you remember Mr. Rathbone? Well he is in the army on an O.C.T.U., and is going through the 'Blitz Course' at Penmaenmawr this week. He came on leave today, and doesn't like the prospect, as one of our boys, an ex-chorister who I can remember, was accidentally shot through the head whilst there, as they use real ammunition.[93]

---

[92] Michael recalled that common weather conditions for Oxford, during the 1940s, included a low lying misty, foggy cloud that would lie in the bowl of Oxford for long periods of time. Michael was convinced that this was another factor that helped to protect Oxford from air raids during the war.

[93] No records have been found to corroborate this story or to identify the ex-chorister.

He tells me that they have to wade through an icy river while depth-charges are being exploded in it. I think it's a bit thick sending men of his age into that place, don't you?

Well, I think that's all I've got to say, so goodbye!

From your loving son, Shirley.

V ••• —

FIXTURES – RUGBY. WEDNESDAY MCS v Old Boys. *The Oxford Times*, Friday 19th November 1943

Sunday [5th December 1943]

Dear Mummy and Daddy,

This morning shortly after breakfast, I happened to go outside for a short time, I heard the sound of a lot of planes, and, lo and behold! I saw 40 fortresses[94]; they were followed by more and more, and in half

---

[94] The Boeing B-17 Flying Fortress was a four-engine heavy bomber primarily used by the United States Army Air Corps.

an hour I counted over 250; I don't know where they had come from, but somewhere must have had a terrific raid.[95]

On my way back from choir, I had a great treat: a 'Centaur' tank was pulled up on Magdalen Bridge, and I spent at least 20 minutes looking over it; also I got half-way into an armoured car.[96]

Thank you for the P.O. for 2/6d; I will most probably store some of it up, so as to buy presents.

As to what I would like for Christmas here are a few 'possibilities'.

(i) 'Staffordshire' by Arthur Mee. 9/6 (?), or

(ii) 'Britain's Glorious navy'[97] 7/6d, or

(iii) 'With Pennants Flying'[98] 9/6
(number 3 is a book about tanks, but it is printed on rotten paper), or

(iv) A good board game, or

(v) 'The Royal Air Force' (a Dumpy Book) or any other 'Dumpy Book' I do not already possess.

I will be perfectly satisfied with one book, so don't worry about getting any more.

---

[95] Michael had witnessed the returning planes from the first bombing run of the 'Crossbow Operations Against Ski Sites', which began on the 5th December 1943. Ski sites were the ski jump like launch sites that the Germans initially used to launch the V1 flying bombs.

[96] The Centaur tank was produced locally. Morris Motors, Cowley was one of seven companies contracted to build Centaur and Cromwell tanks to help Leyland Motors and Birmingham Railway Carriage and Wagon Company meet production targets during the war.

[97] *Britain's Glorious Navy*, Ed. Reginald H.S. Bacon, Odhams Press; 1943.

[98] *With Pennants Flying, The Immortal Deeds of the Royal Armoured Corps*, David Masters, Eyre & Spottiswoode, 1943.

Exams start on Wednesday, and I am very busy 'swotting up', so goodbye and T.T.F.N.

From, Shirley.

V ••• —

The skull and crossbones doddle at the end of this letter.

Men looking over a Centaur Tank built by Morris Motors, Cowley, Oxford, 1943

Towards the end of November and start of December 1943, Oxford was hit by an influenza epidemic that necessitated the deployment of

the Civil Defence organisation and the help of the WVS to aid the supply of domestic services and food to those that were incapacitated. Army doctors were not available to help the overburdened civilian doctors, so a request was made to employers to not demand a Medical Certificates for absence.

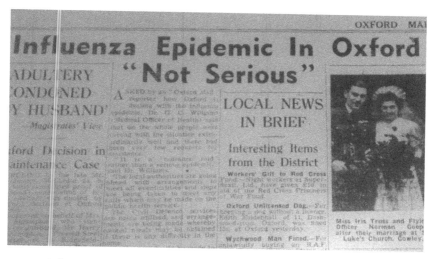

Influenza Epidemic In Oxford 'Not Serious'. *Oxford Mail*, Wednesday 15th December 1943.

Spring (Hilary) Term 1944

Tuesday [1st February 1944]

Dear Mummy and Daddy,

I'm very sorry that I didn't write on Sunday, I should have done, and there is no excuse.

On Sunday I went to a big concert in the Sheldonian. Mr Taylor was playing the organ there, so he took some of us into the organ-loft free! (The cheapest seats were 3/6!). The programme was a Vaughan Williams Mass and Part of 'Samson', which needless to say, I enjoyed very much. They sang 'Let the Bright Seraphim', with Orchestra, and it sounded very fine.

Could you please hurry up with my Costume for the play? Mr Greenham would like the costumes ready in about a fortnight.[99]

I am very pleased with my J.T.C. battledress, but I haven't worn it on parade yet, as they are having an old pair of army boots 'done up' for me, and they will be cheap and without coupons.

I have got a smart little lapel badge to wear when in mufti. It is silver and blue.

May I remind you again to please send my bicycle-lamp with a new battery in, please? I need a torch very badly nowadays, because it is dark when we come back from choir.

The weather is very springy, but gets cold in the afternoons.

To-day I had my tinned perch, but I'm not very thrilled with them.

To-morrow I hope to see 'The Four Feathers', which is showing at Oxford.

Our form-master says it is very good, and I am willing to pay 2/3d to get in.

Please excuse my ghastly writing, as I'm in a fearful hurry.

From your loving son, Shirley.

P.S. Please thank Aunty Berny very much for the cake; tell her I'll be writing as soon as poss.

---

[99] Michael played the part of the Duchess de la Trémouille in the school's adaptation of St Joan, 25-28th March 1944.

MUSIC IN OXFORD. SHELDONIAN
CONCERT. *The Oxford Times*,
Friday 4th February 1944.

THE FOUR FEATHERS. *Oxford Mail*,
Saturday 29th January 1944.

THE FOUR FEATHERS. *Oxford Mail*,
Tuesday 1st February 1944.

Monday [14th February 1944]

Dear Mummy and Daddy,

I'm very sorry that I am late with my letter again; I wrote a letter on Sunday but forgot to post it, I think, but I am in good health etc, so don't worry.

Last Sunday I went out to Godstow, and tried to get tea at the 'Trout' inn, but it was too early.[100]

While I was waiting outside the inn, who should I meet but John Titley, the boy who stayed at the 'Why not?'.

Thank you very much indeed for the parcel, which I enjoyed very much.

Could you please send me that Communion book which Daddy promised me? At the present I have been issued with a very high-church thing called 'St. Christopher's Prayer Book' filled with lots of Blessed Virgin Mary stuff, and I would like to be brought up in the Church of England. The confirmation is near the end of next month.[101]

Only 47 days and I'll be home again!

Your loving son, Shirley

Sunday [27th February 1944]

Dear Mummy and Daddy,

Well, it is the first Sunday in Lent once more, and I enclose my two – penny bit, which was given to me just now, in Chapel.

Remember to put it in the little boot! This will be my fourth one, I think.

Yesterday afternoon I watched our first four row against an Old Boy's four and beat them by a length.

I did not go to the Varsity Rugger Match because it was quite cold, and anyway, they are only 'scratch teams'.

I am looking forward very much to your stay; it will be nice for you to come and see the play. Mr. Greenham and Mr. Elam have accepted the frocks and thank you very much for the kind gift.

---

[100] Godstow is approximately a 4 ½ mile walk from the school.
[101] The Confirmation service was held on Saturday 25th March 1944 (Lady Day) and conducted by The Bishop of Dorchester.

I paraded for the first time in uniform[102] on Friday at J.T.C.. My tunic is about three sizes too big and I am having it changed.

Having missed two days last week, I was 21st in form.

From your loving son, Shirley

FEBRUARY, 1944

The Oxford University Rugby XV., who defeated Cambridge University on the Iffley-road ground, Oxford, on Saturday.

The Oxford University Rugby XV, who defeated Cambridge University on the Iffley Road ground, Oxford, on Saturday. *Oxford Mail*, Monday 28th February 1944.

---

[102] The uniforms issued to the boys of the J.T.C. were from the First World War School Cadet Corps and many boys could not stand the roughness of the material. Peter Shier (OW, 1940-45) remembers wearing his pyjamas underneath to protect his skin.

Monday [6th March 1944]

Dear Mummy and Daddy,

Thank you very much for the P.O. which arrived Saturday evening.

Yesterday I had a fine time. I went to the Stations with three other boys, and we were allowed in the engine-sheds and all over the goods-yards. I went in Diesel streamlined engines, American engines, express engines, tank engines, and goods engines.

I spent all afternoon there, and had a grand time.

Thank you also for the eggs, which I have now finished.

I will not see much of you on the day before Confirmation, as I will be on some exercise stunt done by the J.T.C., at Glymton [sp. Glympton] Park, near Woodstock.[103] This will take all morning and afternoon but I can come out with you in the evening.

By the way, have I enough coupons for a pair of heavy boots, for J.T.C.? Of course, I can wear them ordinarily, of course, and they would be extremely useful.

Also, have you got my Personal Points? They are not at school here, so I suppose that they must be at home, and it is annoying to go without sweets.

We have got a J.T.C. 'Field-Day' on Friday, and I am quite looking forward to it.

I had better be closing down now, or I'll be missing the post.

So goodbye from

Your loving son, Shirley

P.S. Did you get the 2d bit safely?

---

[103] The Glympton Park exercise was on Friday 24th March 1944

The school magazine, *The Lily*, of July 1944 reported that 'The production [of St Joan] deserves high praise, particularly when one remembers the difficulties of clothing coupons …'. The cast list includes the Duchess de la Tremouille played by S. Hickey. The *Oxford Mail* also praised the 'colour and interest' added by the costumes and reported 'All the boys spoke their lines extremely well.'

SCHOOLBOYS PLAY '*ST. JOAN*' AT OXFORD.
Oxford Mail, Monday 27th March 1944.

Saturday [11th March 1944]

Dear Mummy and Daddy,

Here's this week's letter on time – what a miracle!?

This afternoon I actually coxed a boat! There was a race on main river (The Isis) and Matron wanted to see it. However, no proper coxes were available, and I, a staunch member of the Hockey Club, and who have never coxed in my life, was called upon! However, I fulfilled my duties without mishap, and Matron, the precious cargo, was delivered safely.[104]

Our 1st IV won its race by 7 lengths or more. The opponents were the Oxford and Worcester Boy's Club.[105]

I think that 'Bim' is a wonderful name for the new member of the family – 'Bim End' is the school's nickname for our study, and all members of our happy family are honoured to know that they are not forgotten.

Yesterday, I had my first 'Field-day'. I wore my nice new battle-dress, and fired a rifle (blank cartridges) at 'enemy troops' who were attacking us up a hill. It was grand fun – just like a game with Brian Higgs, only a bit more serious, and with a real service rifle instead of a stick as my weapon.

Thank you very much indeed for the P.O. and ration-book, which were both gratefully accepted.

It is not bad weather now, and the crocuses are out on the lawns. I think the news just now is very heartening, and I read the newspapers every day. All the school is buzzing with rumours – the best one is that the railways will only be carrying troops after next week and that we will all be packed home in advance! However we have heard nothing yet.

I was 20th in the form last week. Please give Bim my best wishes, and cherio from your loving son, Shirley.

Rumour of an imminent Allied invasion of Europe was understandably rife in the Spring of 1944. The Oxford population were told it would be unpatriotic to travel by train over the summer months, the train network being required for the fast movement of troops, based around the country, to the disembarkation ports on the south coast

---

[104] This taxi service for matron would have taken her from School House half a mile down the Cherwell River to The Isis.
[105] The Oxford and Worcester Boy's Club was based in St Clement close to the school.

and for the resupply of the invasion force with food and equipment. General Montgomery, commander of the 21st Army Group, was also seen in Oxford in mid-April 1944 consulting with amongst other people, Sir Henry Tizard, the then President of Magdalen College and chairman of the Aeronautical Research Committee, only six weeks before D-Day.

Sir Henry Tizard, President of Magdalen College, showing Gen. Montgomery round during the General's visit to Oxford. *Oxford Mail*, Thursday 20th April 1944

With the war in its closing stages and a new era anticipated by many, the *Oxford Mail* announced that the Headmaster of MCS, Mr Kennard Davis, would be retiring at the end of the term, after fourteen years of Headship. By this time, Kennard Davis had already received the sad news of the death of fifty old boys of the school due to the war, relaying the sobering stories to the school community via assemblies and the school magazine. Of the fifty, Davis had taught thirty-four of these boys personally. The stress and strain of this loss no doubt contributed to his decision to step down for a 'younger man [who] should take over [ready] for the post-war period'. The school would eventually lose seventy-four of its alumni as a result of the Second World War, a significant number considering the small size of the school in the pre-war era, when it was only ever approximately 170 strong.

'DO NOT TRAVEL IN JULY AND AUGUST': Oxford Told Overcrowding in Trains May be Intolerable. *Oxford Mail*, Friday 28th April 1944.

Magdalen College School Head Retiring. *Oxford Mail*, Thursday 20th April 1944.

Summer (Trinity) Term 1944

In the summer of 1944 Michael became Head Chorister and premier solo boy. His voice never 'broke' as many boys' do, but very slowly dropped pitch until he passed his sixteenth birthday whereupon he was granted a generous bursary by the college enabling him to stay on at the school until he was nearly eighteen.

In the following letter Michael apologises for not writing to his parents the previous week, giving as his excuse a lack of writing paper and little spare time. In actual fact, on the Monday (May Day) Michael and his friend Barry Lyndon had ' ... 'borrowed' the Master's punt and persuaded an Egyptian boy, Farouk Abdul Nabi, to join us on our own outing, during which Nabi (who couldn't swim) fell in the river. We dragged him out and smuggled him back into the boarding house, hoping to dry his clothes on radiators before our sins were detected. As it was the summer term there was no heating and we were quickly discovered. There was only one outcome and we were soundly beaten by the Master himself, an occasion for much morbid spectator interest as we were closely watched as we left the Master's study; it was considered bad form to show signs of pain; Barry and I managed to suppress our anguish but Farouk the Egyptian gratified the audience with a noisy display of hysterics.'

Sunday [7th May 1944]

Dear Mummy and Daddy,

I am very sorry that I did not write last Sunday, but I couldn't get this paper till Monday, and what little spare time I have has been given up to writing to Aunty Brenda and Uncle Shirley and playing cricket.

Well, now I am started, I will tell you my story from the beginning: After an eventful journey, (I had to change at Risborough), I arrived at Uncle Shirley's in time for tea. Uncle Shirley, by the way, was waiting for me at the station with a wheelbarrow, into which I put my case!

When I arrived at Grove House, I washed, took off my jacket, and had tea on the loggia. After tea Uncle Shirley and I went to see Butler's Court,[106] a magnificent, but now rather moth eaten place in my opinion, as the Frenchmen have let the garden go to ruin. The big room is a recreation room, where sailors lie sprawled on the couches

---

[106] Butlers Court, Beaconsfield (designed by Arthur Vernon to be a retired gentleman's residence, was built in 1891) was owned by Shirley Timmis, and during the Second World War it became a Red Cross hospital for men of the French navy. After the war the building remained unused until 1956 when it was purchased by a paper-making firm. Eventually, in 2012 the building was returned to its original grandeur as part of a property development.

lazing the time away, when they could be helping to keep the grounds tidy. They are disgusting, these Frenchmen, and Uncle Shirley doesn't like them either. The place is in such a mess that Uncle Shirley is leaving it for good, as he says that it will take ten to fifteen years to clean it up, and by then he will be dead.

Then we went to the farm. There, there is a lovely goat called Dinah, which followed me around like a dog, and tried to eat my hankerchief!

There are lots of little piglets, who were very funny, and a gaggle of goslings. Also I saw the pedigree cows. Aren't they fine?

Having done that, we went back to the house, and I helped Aunt Brenda in the garden till dinner, after which I went to bed. I spent all next morning at 'Bekonscot', where I helped to lay out the aerodrome. I was thrilled with it, and wandered around in a sort of dazed wonder.

Uncle Shirley and I dined together off salmon; Aunt Brenda (in F.A.N.Y.)[107] uniform, had gone to London after breakfast, and Uncle Shirley saw me off at the station by himself. I got a through train to Oxford, and got in at about 2.30, 15/- the richer!

On May-Day I went out in a canoe with Lyndon Mi. We took our lunch with us, and we went as far as Parson's Pleasure.[108]

---

[107] The First Aid Nursing Yeomanry is a British independent all-female registered charity formed in 1907 and was active in both nursing and intelligence work during the First and Second World Wars. In September 1938, the FANY Corps was also asked to form the initial Motor Driver Companies of the Auxiliary Territorial Service, called the Women's Transport Service. The FANY was officially renamed the Princess Royal's Volunteer Corps in 1999 and is now referred to as FANY (PRVC).

[108] Parson's Pleasure, in the University Parks at Oxford, was a secluded male-only nude bathing location on the River Cherwell. Traditionally it was also the site where MCS held its swimming sports during the summer months at the turn of the twentieth century. Also referred to as Cox's because the proprietor of the bathing place for more than seventy-five years, until his death in 1917, was Charles Cox. The facility was finally closed by the council in 1991.

Today I went to Aunty Effie's for lunch and tea with Lyndon Mi., and had a jolly good time.

One of the boys in our study has actually <u>given</u> me a small microphone, which I'm very pleased with. We have radio communications with one of the other studies, but we have only one pair of ear-phones. Geoff Brereton used to have a pair, if he has still got them he <u>might</u> want to sell them. Could you possibly communicate with him, and, if he is willing, buy them and send them directly to me?

I am now feeling rather exhausted, so goodbye,

From your loving son, Shirley.

Bekonscot (in Beaconsfield), where Michael visited and helped to layout the aerodrome during his stay with his Uncle Shirley and Aunty Brenda in May 1944, is the oldest original model village in the world. It was created by Roland Callingham in the late 1920s and it portrays aspects of England mostly dating from the 1930s.

Bekonscot model village. The aerodrome. c.1944

Oxford Salute the Soldier Week 1944

In 1944 the Government launched a national savings scheme called 'Salute the Soldier Week' to help fund and equip the British Army in readiness for the final phase of the war, when the Allies would have to take on the German Army in land battles across Europe and into Germany itself. For Oxford, the Salute the Soldier week began on Saturday 13th May 1944 and, like previous Government fundraising weeks included parades, exhibitions and other war paraphernalia. Many local institutions set themselves targets to motivate their communities to donate. MCS raised the sum of £877 15s. 6d. after having set itself the target of £500.

Oxford Mail, Monday 8th May 1944	*Oxford Mail*, Friday 12th May 1944	*Oxford Mail*, Friday 12th May 1944

Oxford youngsters had a royal time in operating one of the anti-aircraft guns on show in St Giles' in connection with 'Salute the Soldier' week.
Oxford Mail, Friday 12th May 1944

Manipulating a twin Bren anti-aircraft gun, one of the popular 'Salute the Soldier' Week thrills for a young visitor to the Therm House Exhibition.
Oxford Mail, Friday 12th May 1944

An incident in the baseball match on Christ Church ground, Oxford, on Saturday, between two American Army teams, staged for the benefit of Oxford's 'Salute the Soldier' Week.
Oxford Mail, Monday 22nd May 1944

The band of H.M.S. Excellent which led Oxford's 'Salute the Soldier' week procession, followed by a contingent of naval ratings from H.M.S. Excellent [at The Plain, with the Victoria Fountain in the background]. *Oxford Mail*, Friday 12th May 1944

The band of Members of the 6th (Oxford City) Battalion Home Guard, led by Commanding Officer, Lieut.-Col. J.A. Douglas at the Plain during Oxford's great 'Salute the Soldier' Week procession, which happily coincided with the Home Guard's fourth birthday. *Oxford Mail*, Friday 12th May 1944

The Mayor of Oxford (Counc. H.C. Ingle) inspecting the contingent of Oxford-born men of the Oxf. And Bucks Light Infty., who took part in the 'Salute the Soldier' Week procession. *Oxford Mail*, Friday 12th May 1944

The commanding officer with the Mayor is believed to be Major John Howard who, a few weeks later was taking part in D-Day, leading the daring glider raid to capture Pegasus Bridge. Major Howard, who served as a policeman in Oxford before the war, became one of Britain's greatest war heroes after he and his men captured 'Pegasus' bridge from the Germans in the early hours of D-Day, 6th June 1944. His story was immortalised in the film The Longest Day. Howard survived the war, despite being wounded. He died in 1999 and is buried at St Michael and All Angels Church in Clifton Hampden.

Sunday [14th May 1944]

Dear Mummy and Daddy,

Yesterday, 'Salute the Soldier' week began in Oxford; the target is £1,250,000, which will probably be reached.

I am writing to you just before going to see the great procession, and a major-general will take the salute. Yesterday, I fired 24 shots with a practice rifle at the exhibition in [T]Herm House.[109]

(after the Parade)

The parade I have just seen <u>was</u> a parade. It lasted just under an hour, and it is estimated that over 50,000 people watched it. Four platoons of our J.T.C. (not ours, thank goodness) marched with Bren guns, Sten guns, and rifles. Just now, outside the school, several thousand people are jammed in a huge crowd, which is slowly melting away.

Have you seen Geoff Brereton about the earphones yet? If you could possibly get me a pair, it would be lovely, as I could, in the holidays, rig up a house telephone (one way).

I have found out that Commem. is on the 17th June, but unless you are very lucky, you won't be able to get in at the Eastgate; it's too late, but there's no harm in trying.

---

[109] Therm House was home to the office and showrooms for Oxford and District Gas Company at 117 and 118 St Aldate's Street, Oxford.

I hope that Uncle Shirley got my letter, which was written a fortnight ago.

I have not made any spectacular cricket scores yet, my highest so far being six.

Not much more news, so goodbye, from your loving son, Shirley.

P.S. I have a solo tonight in Haydn's 'Creation' called 'On thee each living soul awaits'.

After almost five years of war, the mix of local, everyday news and global war news became familiar partners on the front of local newspapers such as the *Oxford Mail* and *The Oxford Times*. It was this local newspaper newsfeed, as much as national newspapers, that was crucial for adults and school boys alike to stay abreast of the progress of the war. What appeared on the front of the *Oxford Mail* on Friday 19th May 1944 was to shock the city and the nation and was to become infamous through the retelling of its story in the film, The Great Escape.

47 Allied Airmen Shot Dead In Mass Escape Bid. *Oxford Mail*, Friday 19th May 1944
[Although the mass escape and killings had taken place in March 1944, news did not reach the Allied Governments until after a routine inspection of the camp in April had been given the information]

With the largest maritime invasion in history about to take place in Normandy, life in Oxford continued with some normality, as can be seen from the 'get-away' rush on the Whitsun bank holiday weekend of 1944. Despite the requests to avoid using the overcrowded rail system, Oxford 'factory workers' flocked to the trains to take the opportunity of returning to their family homes for the long Whitsuntide weekend break.

HOLIDAY RUSH AT OXFORD STATIONS. *Oxford Mail*, Saturday 27th May 1944

Noticeable in Michael's letters home is a palpable anticipation and excitement for the imminent invasion of France (for instance, see 11th March letter: 'All the school is buzzing with rumours'). Michael and the other boys were reading the newspapers every day and the run of headlines in the *Oxford Mail* during the summer term of 1944, reporting the progress being made in Italy and the increased intensity of bombing raids on France, fuelled that schoolboy excitement.

Pre-Invasion Blitz Launched against French Coast To-day? *Oxford Mail*,
Thursday 25th May 1944

ANZIO MEN 16 ½ MILES FROM ROME. *Oxford Mail*, Monday 29th May 1944

GERMANS' LAST LINE BEFORE ROME CRACKING. *Oxford Mail*,
Wednesday 31st May 1944

ALLIES LAND IN FRANCE. *Oxford Mail*, Tuesday 6th June 1944

ALLIES LAND IN NORMANDY. *Oxford Mail*, Tuesday 6th June 1944

FIFTY MILES OF COAST OCCUPIED. *Oxford Mail*, Wednesday 7th June 1944

Sunday [11th June 1944]

Dear Mummy and Daddy,

As you can guess, I am very excited about Saturday; the prize-giving will, unfortunately be in Big School, not the College Dining Hall. I saw Mr Blackwell yesterday; he seems glad that I've got a prize.[110]

Everyone was very excited on Tuesday, or rather, 'D day'. All the time, large formations of American planes are passing overhead, a particularly large bunch going over at 5.30 this morning. I expect you have seen planes covered with stripes like this:-

Well, all planes in the invasion air force are painted thus, and we have seen plenty of them.

Thank you very much indeed for the parcel; I enjoyed the mince-pies and sponge-cake very much. I will try to write to Uncle Hilton to-day, or to-morrow.

I hope you like my new note-paper having already exhausted my old pool. Yesterday I made a great decision and got four bob's worth of papers and envelopes with crests; altogether a good bargain; seeing that it is all in a strong cardboard box.

I have recently purchased, from other boys, two Bren Gun Carriers and a lorry, for my tin soldier army, plus a naval gun on wheels.

---

[110] Michael was jointly awarded the A.E. Cowley Prize, for the senior Chorister soloists, along with his friend Ken Morley.

My money is still alright, as I have about 16/- left, owing to the fact that I dumped a pound in the House-Master's care at the beginning of term.[111]

On Friday night we are singing 'Blessing, Glory, Wisdom and Thanks' by Bach, and to-night at 8.30, we are singing madrigals in the cloisters. I will show you the programme next week.

There is a bus for High Wycombe on Monday at 10 a.m. This is the first bus of the day.

From your very excited son, Shirley.

On Saturday 17th June, at the annual presentation of prizes at MCS, Michael found out that the new headmaster (Master) of MCS was to be his Classics teacher, the then deputy headmaster (Usher) of the school, Bob Stanier.

MAGDALEN COLLEGE SCHOOL, OXFORD: New Headmaster Announced at Prize-giving and Sports.
Picture right: A large crowd attended the Magdalen College School annual sports on Saturday. Photo shows a scene during a long jump event.
Oxford Mail, Monday 19th June 1944.

---

[111] The Master and House Master kept charge of the boarders pocket money provided by the parents, and boys had to ask for it each time it was needed. Detailed questions about why it was needed had to be answered before it was given over.

Sunday [25th June 1944]

Dear Mummy and Daddy,

It is a filthy day to-day, and I am staying in till the weather improves, which does not seem likely. Thursday we had the half-holiday promised by Mr. Blackwell at Commem.; as it was a very fine day, I went to the baths for the first swim of the season. I only stayed in for half an hour, but I think that's quite enough for the first time.

I have been given a piece of a buzz-bomb[112] by Morley, who had one a couple of hundred yards from his house near Guildford.[113]

The Paibas (those people with the three boys, who stayed at the Eastgate) had one only fifty yards away, which broke the ceilings and windows, and made the walls bulge alarmingly.[114]

Mr and Mrs Lyndon were walking down their road when a buzz-bomb went just over their heads.[115] They threw themselves under a hedge and the thing went off a few dozen yards away. They went to assist the rescue people, and Mrs Lyndon had to take charge of a woman who kept on fainting. Lyndon minor is spending the holiday in Gloucestershire but other boys may not be so lucky.[116] It certainly knocks on the head any chance of seeing Jean next vac.

---

[112] Buzz bomb was the name given to the German V1 flying bomb. The first buzz bomb was fired at London on 13th June 1944, with eventually just less than ten thousand being fired at South-East England over the following four months. The attacks tailed off from August and were stopped for good in October as tactics for destroying them in the air became better and the launch sites on the French coast were slowly overrun by the allies. One last V1 was to land at Datchworth in Hertfordshire on 29th March 1945, fired from a V1 launch site in the Low Countries.

[113] Ken Morley's home was actually in West Horsley, Leatherhead, Surrey.

[114] Denis, Michael and Henry Paiba's home was 4 Grosvenor, Gardens, Willesden Green, NW2.

[115] The Lyndons lived at 7 Florence Road, Sanderstead, South Croydon, CR2.

[116] Rather than return to their home town or city during the summer vacation and be at risk from German bombs, many boys went to summer 'harvest camps' in Somerset and Gloucestershire. This also helped with the labour shortage on farms. David Trebilcock, a contemporary of Michael's remembered that flax-pulling and the wheat harvest were common tasks during these summers.

Could you please send me 2/6d for subscriptions to a farewell party for Mr Davis?

Great news! I have been chosen to play Ophelia in the Dramatic Society's production of Hamlet next year. I have made a start now!

Also, I am doing the Title-rôle in 'Billy, the man-catching tiger' a play which some of us are 'doing' on the last evening of term. We are all members of Top Middle and Bim End, with one exception, who is in Top Little.

I rose in form last week to 19th which is a small improvement.

We are seeing more and more jet-planes now; they must be all round us, for one boy saw one on the ground at an aerodrome near Oxford.

Please can you send my autograph album, as there is a big charity Cricket Match next Sunday, with about ten really famous players playing in it. I'm sorry that I have to keep sending for things all the time, but so many things seem to be happening this term.

To-night I am singing my 20th solo of the term, which calls for a spot of mild celebration.

Please keep Bim in good trim and give her a big hug from me.

Love to you both from your loving son, Shirley.

P.S. Has Mr Edgerton got that book yet?

CHIPPY'S STOOP OF ALE. *These doodle appeared at the end of Michael's letter of 25th June 1944.*

A scene at Magdalen Bridge, Oxford – a popular venue for holiday makers.
Oxford Mail, Tuesday 20th June 1944.

In contrast to this tranquil June scene in Oxford, London now became the target of 'Flying Bombs', the V1 (from 13th June to October 1944) and then rockets, the V2 (from 8th September 1944 to 27th March 1945) launched from France and the Low Countries, causing great death and devastation and sufficient concern to produce the third mass evacuation of the war from the capital.

**FLYING BOMB HITS HOSPITAL WING:
Seven Bodies Found: Other Patients
Missing.** Two more hospitals in Southern
England were among buildings hit or
damaged by flying bomb blast during the
night and early day.
Oxford Mail, Saturday 1st July 1944.

More Flying Bombs Blown Up In Air.
Oxford Mail, Monday 3rd July 1944.

**FLYING BOMB DEATHS ONE PER BOMB – Premier: 2,754 LAUNCED; 8,000 PEOPLE
INJURED: Great Destruction of Rocket Sites.**
Oxford Mail, Thursday 6th July 1944.

Sunday 2nd July [1944]

Dear Mummy and Daddy,

Well, to make up for my last short letter, here is an extra long one.

Last Sunday I saw some really top-line cricket. A team from an Airborne division played an R.A.F. group on our field. Playing for the R.A.F. was Bartlett of Surrey and England, and Griffiths [sp. Griffith], England's fast bowler, who played wicket-keeper. Bartlett and Griffiths both gave me their autographs at which I was very pleased. Also, last Sunday, the choristers played New College Choir, and lost. I made 0 not out (!)

Before the match started, I gave a deceased baby shrew a military funeral.

At the moment, I am the proud possessor of a jar-full of water snails; captured them this morning to study their habits.

The other day, I saw a jet-plane and made a rough drawing of it. It looks something like this:

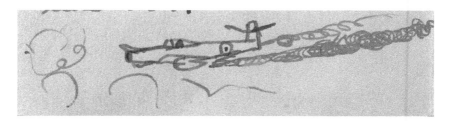

It leaves a double trail of dark vapour behind it, and is it fast?!*.

Has Mr. Edgerton got that railway book yet? The new edition is out at last, so could you please ask him to give it to Daddy when it arrives?

Also: has Mr Spencer got that tank book?

We have had one or two sirens recently, but nothing has happened.

Please remember the collects!

As I was absent, I was not placed properly in form this week.

From your loving son,

Shirley

P.S. I'm including the photographs[117] of the dramatic society. I am in the big crowd, fourth from right. I was taken without part of my costume, which was being used as a flag in Scene 1, so pardon me for looking such a sight!

Big Group. L to R

Dobereiner, Wayneric, Wilson, Gulliver, Nabi, self, Byk, Goldstein, Stoneham.

Small Group. L to R.

Spence, White, Gulliver, Lane, Metcalfe.

Hugh Bartlett and Billy Griffith who gave their autographs to Michael had, less than three weeks earlier, taken part in the D-Day glider landings in Normandy. Hugh Bartlett played cricket for Surrey between 1933-1935, but played for Sussex either side of the War. He never played for England, but was an effective attacking left handed batsman. During the Second World War, Bartlett was commissioned into the Royal Army Service Corps, and then transferred to the Royal West Kent Regiment in 1942, before serving in the Glider Pilot Regiment and eventually becoming second-in-command to Billy Griffith. Bartlett served at Normandy, Arnhem and in the Rhine crossings. 'Billy' Stewart Cathie Griffith and Hugh Bartlett were close friends. They had been at Dulwich College and Cambridge together, and both started their careers at Surrey. Despite Griffith being in the shadow of Bartlett while at Dulwich, it was Griffith, a wicket-keeper, who toured with the MCC in 1935 and 1936 and went on to captain Sussex and play three Test matches for England in 1948 and 1949. Griffith was commissioned into the Officers Training Corps in 1938, and transferred to the Royal Army Service Corps in 1939, later serving in the Glider Pilot Regiment. He had the honour of carrying the

---

[117] At the time of going to print these photographs had not been rediscovered.

commander of the 6th Airborne Division, Major-General 'Windy' Gale into Normandy on 6th June 1944, crash landing after being caught in a storm. He also took part in the Battle of Arnhem.

Monday [10th July 1944]

Dear Mummy and Daddy,

I'm sorry that I did not write yesterday, as I was swotting for Exams (which start to-day) in the morning, and went to the Clapperton's in the afternoon, where I had a narrow squeak, as a full sized viper attacked me; while I held the dog back with one hand, and kicked the snake. Mr Clapperton slew it. I am glad to say that I was not hurt, but it was a very narrow escape.

Exams start today and everyone is very excited.

I won't do excellently in Maths, but I am sure of my Latin, especially Caesar, which is a 'sitter'.

I'm afraid I <u>must</u> ask for a spot of money for the last 10 days (would 5/- be too much?).

I have done a portrait of our form-master, and he is very pleased with it, as he wants to show it to his wife.

I must close down now, as it is 9 o'clock, so goodbye from your 'getting more excited' son, Shirley.

As Michael reaches adolescence and starts to mature into a young man, his letters reveal small indications of him adopting and evolving his own style. For instance, until now he had written all his capital D's as taught, with ornate curls. In July 1944, he appears to have made a definite decision to change this style of D to a less ornate and simple D, as highlighted by his writing of 'Daddy' at the start of each of his letters. This would be a style of D he would use for the rest of his life. Less than eighteen months later, in 1946, he would make the biggest change to his image by dropping the use of his first name, Shirley, and adapting the use his of his middle name 'Michael' as his preferred signature.

Dear Mummy and Daddy.
Sunday 2nd July 1944

Dear Mummy and Daddy.
Monday 10th July 1944

Sunday [16th July 1944]

Dear Mummy and Daddy,

Well, again I am writing the last letter of term, and getting very excited about it.

This next week will be a grand one, as the choristers will be having choir teas etc. galore.

Last night, however, we had gaudy, my first one, as I was in bed last year. There is not space enough for me to tell you all about it, except that I, the new head chorister, sang the Latin grace, and that I had peaches, grapes, claret and concentrated white wine. As is the old custom, several, if not all the choristers stuffed their pockets with fruit and brought it back for the boarders. I used a sponge bag as a receptacle for peaches, cherries, apples, grapes and huge gooseberries.

I did pretty well in exams coming 7th in Latin, 8th in English, and getting over 50% for almost every other paper.

I'm simply longing to see Bim again; she must have almost forgotten me by now, I expect.

Also, what's more, I am in the best of health, no trace of cough or anything; I have only been to the baths twice this term, and haven't been in the river or Tumbling Bay.[118] Still, I hope to pay regular visits to Cowley Baths.

I will see about getting my ticket tomorrow, and will send luggage etc., per LMS.

---

[118] Tumbling Bay bathing place is a former open air swimming pool on a backwater of the Thames near Botley Park in Oxford. A pair of weirs maintains a constant water level in the swimming pool between them. Tumbling Bay was used as a bathing place for almost two hundred years until it was closed by Oxford City Council in 1990.

I am starting to pack up my things to day, so goodbye (for the last time)!

From Shirley

Whoopee

V • • • —

Yoicks

Autumn 1944 – Summer 1945

Stout, Fire, Frost and Victory

Five years after blackout regulations had been imposed in Britain (1st September 1939) the likelihood of aerial raids by Germany had been reduced to the point that a 'Dim-out' was introduced in September 1944, which allowed lighting to the equivalent of moonlight. Michael therefore returned to Oxford in September 1944 for his sixth year at MCS and for the first time without blackout restrictions. A full Blackout would be imposed if an alert was sounded. Full lighting of streets was allowed in April 1945.

Getting ready for the 'light-up' – Corporation workmen are now engaged in putting Oxford's street lighting in order for the relaxation of the black-out restrictions.
Oxford Mail, Saturday 9th September 1944

Details of the air raids on Oxfordshire, from the start of the war to February 1944, were released to the public in a newspaper report in January 1945 (*Oxford Mail*, 6th January 1945). The divulgence of this report suggests the threat from further air raids had passed and indicates that Oxford's avoidance from bombing was as much to do with fortune as it was to do with German planning, with nearby towns Witney, Thame, Kidlington and Bicester all being hit.[119] Many theories have emerged to explain why Oxford escaped bombing during the war including that Hitler had identified Oxford for his capital or command centre after an invasion of England. However, Michael offered his own thoughts on this, having experienced the weather in Oxford first hand during the war. He said that typical and frequent weather conditions for Oxford, during the 1940s, included a low lying misty, foggy cloud that would lie in the bowl of Oxford[120] for long periods of time. His experience of these weather conditions and his ultimate experience as a military pilot, seeing combat in the Korean war, convinced him that this blanket cover of Oxford would have made precision bombing of Oxford's industrial sites such as Morris Motors (who manufactured the de Havilland Tiger Moth training airplane and repaired other damaged aircraft) and the Osberton Radiator Company (who made radiators and other parts for the Spitfire aircraft), and military targets including the Slade and Cowley Camps, surprisingly difficult, easily aborted, or conveniently switched at last minute to nearby, more visible targets.

---

[119] Interestingly the Oxfordshire districts which sustained the most prolonged bombing of the war were those of Weston-on-the-Green (where there was an airfield which was used by various RAF Squadrons and Training Units/Schools), Chesterton and Charlton-on-Otmoor which constitute a 3-mile-wide corridor between Kidlington and Bicester (both of which had RAF airfields).

[120] Oxford, with its significant system of low-lying water ways and meadows, sits at an average height of approx. 200ft, surrounded by four main ridges of about or over 500ft above sea level: Boars Hill (to the SW), Shotover Country Park (to the SE), Wytham Woods (to the NW) and Beckley (to the NE).

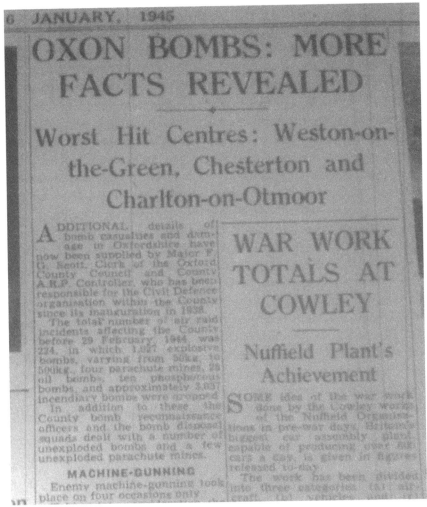

OXON BOMBS: MORE FACTS REVEALED: Worst Hit Centres: Weston-on-the-Green, Chesterton and Charlton-on-Otmoor. 'The total number of air raid incidents affecting the County …. was 224, in which 1,027 explosive bombs, varying from 50Kg to 500Kg, four parachute mines, 28 oil bombs, ten phosphorus bombs and approximately 3,037 incendiary bombs were dropped.'
Oxford Mail, Saturday 6th January 1945

THEY HAD US ON THE LIST. 'The German photograph map of Oxford reproduced above is one of three which an R.A.F. man sent to Mr Bradfield, Barnet Street, Oxford. ... of the other two maps – one of the Morris Motors works at Cowley and the other of part of the works and other targets in the vicinity. ... the photos were taken on the same day – 24 September 1940'.

Oxford Mail, Wednesday 6th June 1945

Autumn (Michaelmas) Term 1944

In September 1944 Bob Stanier became only the third different Master (headmaster) of MCS since the turn of the century. He had already been at the school for nine years, in the role of Usher (deputy headmaster). Although staff stability and constancy were more common place for institutions and organisations during this era, this exceptional loyalty and strong leadership enabled MCS to initially survive then thrive during a period which included two world wars, much financial insecurity (as the College worked to end its financial responsibility for the school) and the necessary reliance on temporary buildings. Stanier was to continue at the helm until 1967, steering MCS to the relative security as a direct grant grammar school (receiving funds from the local education authority). Although still a fee-paying school, the direct grant status meant that 25% of the places could be offered free to local boys and some boarders from neighbouring counties. The school would operate as a direct grant school from 1944 until 1976, when it finally became a private school.

Sunday 24th September 1944

Dear Mummy and Daddy,

Well, we are all settling down now to school life again; I have been promoted to the Upper IV, and have sorrowfully left Bim End, where I am cock of the roast.

There are two new boys in Middle End with whom I am already friends.

Yesterday, I spent the afternoon riding on a bike round Oxford delivering messages for Mr. Stanier.

Mr. Stanier ('Bob') has made a lot of changes, which I will mention next week.

There isn't much time to say anything else, except to say that my pen's safe, and that I've told Matron all the things as directed.

Hoping to tell you more next weekend.

From your loving son, Shirley

How's Bim?

Sunday [22nd October 1944]

Dear Mummy and Daddy,

I was very disappointed when I heard that Bim's litter was still-born. I expect she needs a bit of practice (!)

Yesterday I went to the theatre to see a 'Firth Shephard' play (Arsenic and Old Lace was in the same series). This one was called 'Junior Miss' and is very funny; I think you would both love it, as, although the scene is in New York, the English Cast do not attempt American accents. (By the way, there are some rather questionable jokes in it).[121]

Last week, I had the pleasure of seeing 'Gone with the Wind'. I thought that it is almost too sad for anyone to see it again. Do try to see it if you can, as it is coming round again.

On Wednesday, I hope to sing 'Gratiarum Actio' at the Restoration Supper in the College dining hall.

The week-end after next will be half-term holiday, wherein any boy may go home with written perm. from his parents, but of course, choristers cannot do anything at all.

I hope that Uncle Eric will have his petrol ration for February, as there is then a large 'three-choirs' concert in the town-hall. It would be lovely if you could come to it.

Don't bother yourself about table-cloth and cushion if you can't get them, but the old cushion on the kitchen rocking chair is good enough for my purpose.

Owing to a day's absence I went down to 20th last week but this week my marks are good so my graph will go up.

---

[121] Michael enclosed the programme in the envelope. 'Junior Miss' was at the New Theatre Oxford for five days, from Tuesday 17th October 1944.

Could you possibly send one or two bars of choc.?

I am glad to know that Mummy's arm is better, she <u>must</u> <u>not</u> <u>over-work</u> <u>it</u>!

Love from Shirley.

GONE WITH THE WIND. *Oxford Mail*, Tuesday 3rd October 1944.

JUNIOR MISS.	**Comedy Of Youth At The 'New'.**	**JOAN WHITE** as she appears in *'Junior Miss'* at Oxford's New Theatre

Oxford Mail, Saturday 14th October 1944

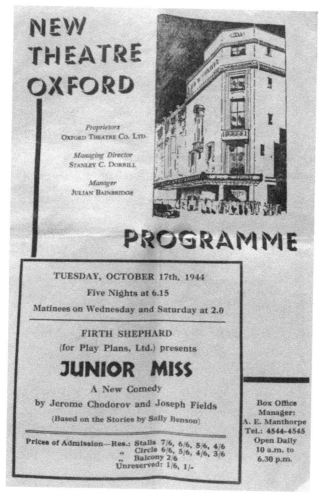

New Theatre Oxford, *Junior Miss* Programme, Tuesday 17th October 1944 for five nights at 6.15pm. Michael enclosed this programme in the envelope with his letter of 22nd October.

Sunday 29th October 1944

Dear Mummy and Daddy,

Before I forget, I must tell you that I am very grateful for the cushion and table-cloth; you are very good to have bought me such a nice cloth, which is the envy of the study. Also thank you for the grub, which was very welcome.

By the way it isn't very long now to the end of term, or rather Xmas Day which is now only 1356 hours distant from the time I write now.

The 1st XV beat 'Oxford Exiles' yesterday 36-3 as you will see in your 'Sunday Times'.

I had a grand time at the College Restoration dinner, where I had:- 2 glasses of claret; ¼ pint of lovely stout, roast chicken, apple + blackberry pie, and lots of other strange and wonderful things.

Tonight I am singing in 'O where shall wisdom be found'.

Did you enjoy 'The way ahead'? On the day I came back I saw David Niven in one of his first films, 'Charge of the Light Brigade' which was very good, though rather bloodthirsty showing a massacre.

On Friday we had a field day, in which I was a Bren-gunner with a dummy bren-gun. A fortnight ago I just failed, by 9 points, to qualify for a second-class shot.

When I missed school last week, I had a head-ache and chill, and my low position of 22nd was explained by the fact that my physics marks were not given in.

Well, goodbye now, with a big tickle for Bim.

From Shirley

No matter whether it was the locally produced Morrell's or the Mackeson's brew that Michael was fed by the College at the Magdalen College Restoration dinner at the tender age of fifteen, the message during the era was that stout was a fortifying drink and would do more good than harm.

 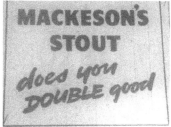

Oxford Mail Advertisements 1944.

THE CHARGE OF THE LIGHT BRIGADE. *The Oxford Times*, Friday 15th September 1944

Tuesday [7th November 1944]

Dear Mummy and Daddy,

I'm very sorry (as usual) that my 'Sunday' letter is a 'Tuesday' letter, but I have had such a busy week-end that I haven't had time for anything like letter writing.

On Saturday I went to the flicks. On Sunday I cycled out to Dorchester with Saunders.[122] On Monday I went to the flicks again. Every evening we played games of 'Murder' in the darkened studies and corridors. Most of the boarders (about 40) had gone home, leaving the choristers and about 10 boarders, with one prefect, in sole possession of the house. What a

---

[122] On several occasions Michael cycled to Dorchester to explore the Wittenham Clumps, a round trip of twenty miles.

good time we had! Also there, was no form order, at least not till tomorrow. My half term report will not be sent home; all reports are being kept by Mr Stanier, who will keep them for future reference.

To-day we started doing trigonometry which seems daft, but I'm not doing badly at it.

I am getting on with my music lessons, but I don't think I like Miss Wiblin nearly as much as Mrs Bear, who is far more personal. I hope I can continue with Music lessons during the vac.

Well goodbye from, Shirley

P.S. Thank you ever so much for the parcel.

Sunday [19ᵗʰ November 1944]

Dear Mummy and Daddy

Thank you very much for the parcel

It has been another somewhat eventless week; On Thursday I went to see the University team's defeat Major Stanley's XV. It was a pretty good match, Oxford at half-time leading 5-0, but they didn't pick up at all, and Stanley's team won 15(?)-5.

Last night, I was informed that, as I am a chorister, I cannot be 'Ophelia' in next term's 'Hamlet'.   I <u>must</u> say that that's a very great encouragement (!). Gosh, if the play is on the same nights as it was last year, it wouldn't interfere at all: I believe Mr. Stanier was responsible for this bit of absurd red tape, moved by some crazy idea.

Well, if they can't get a chorister for Ophelia, they'll be in the hell of a mess, because she has to do plenty of singing, and it won't be exactly pretty to see a gentle lady singing bass.

I must say it was a horrible disappointment, and to-day I'm in the foul temper with everybody. I think I've been the victim of a dirty filthy trick.

Matron has told me to stop indoors to-day, as I have a slight cold, but I don't mind particularly as it is windy and cold.

Last week I was 22ⁿᵈ, a slight improvement.

My love to Bim,

From your loving son. Shirley

P.S. Just because I'm disappointed don't think I'm unhappy.

P.P.S. Has Mummy stopped smoking yet? If she has tell me, because I intend to get her a cigarette-lighter this year.

P.P.P.S. Could you send me an old battered Dinky Toy car from my store - the one I want looks like this,

It is a 'Tootsie Toy'.[123] It is light green.

MAJOR STANLEY'S XV AT OXFORD. *Oxford Mail,* Friday 10th November

OXFORD SIDE'S GOOD WORK. Narrow Margin for Major Stanley's XV. *Oxford Mail,* Friday 17th November 1944.

---

[123] Tootsietoy® still manufactures die cast toy cars and vehicles.

A sign that any lingering threat of invasion had gone and that the war was entering its last phase was the order for the local Home Guard to stand down on the 3rd December 1944. Four and a half years after the first call for enrolment in the initially named Local Defence Volunteers, the stand down of the Home Guard battalions was marked with parades across the country.

Lieut.-Col J.A. Douglas (Officer Commanding the 6th Oxon (Oxford City) Battalion) taking the salute in St. Giles, Oxford at the Home Guard stand-down parade yesterday.
Oxford Mail, Monday 4th December 1944.

Sunday 10th December [1944]

VOLUME 1

Dear Mummy and Daddy,

As the time draws near to my arrival home, thousands of ideas flood my head, and I'm sure that I will forget a lot of them.

First, I have a grievance to utter. As usual I will return on Christmas Day, (Monday), on the usual train but I will only have till January 10th when school starts again. You see, as there was a half-term holiday, a corresponding number of days will be knocked off the holiday; the boarders will have just about three weeks, but you'll only have me at home for a fortnight.

On Friday, exams started. We have already had the Latin and History papers, at which I did alright. Tomorrow is a stiff day, with Physics, French, and Maths Paper I, which will consist of Trigonometry and Geometry.

This afternoon we are having the annual carol service in the ante-chapel, in which I am singing a quartet. To-morrow on the King's accession, we are singing 'Zadok the Priest'.

I am getting a special Xmas card for Bim, with either pictures of cats or mice.

I have got an eye on a useful present for you each, a CENSORED and an DITTO DITTO, they are nice things, aren't they? (Heh-heh, I'll make you guess)

Michael's doodle of Father Christmas

If you like, I'll get some books at Blackwell's and ask them to send them to you and charge them to you also. Can you tell me how much money you want me to spend on books.

Don't worry please about sending me too much money for the extra week, as I can always bring back the change.

The only other person (except you, of course) who is getting anything from me, is my faithful friend Brian [Cairns], to whom I will present an aeroplane kit.

(You could get me one, if you want to; you know the shop. (Bagnall's))

And now, if you turn to Volume two of this letter, I give you a list of 'THINGS I WOULD LIKE'

VOLUME 2.

1. Books (as already arranged)

2. A T-square (from Smith's perhaps)

3. An aeroplane or ship kit. If an aeroplane kit, MUST BE BALSA

4. Money for extra week, (that I will count as a Christmas present)

or

5. A small bookstand to bring back to school next term; this I could buy at home in a second-hand shop.

or

ANY BRIGHT IDEAS

And, of course:- DON'T THINK I EXPECT YOU TO GET ME EVERYTHING ON THE LIST.

At the moment I am sorting out my term's drawings. There is one (I think, my term's best) of the battle of Trafalgar, and sundry ships, tanks, faces, cartoons, portraits, sketches, of which I am only bringing home the best.

I will, in every probability be getting the Ellerton[124] this year, which will prove that I am not the 'black sheep' of the family, also, when I leave the choir, I will receive a pension from College, worth £25 a year; Lucky boy, that Oi Be!

That explosion near Burton must have been awful, judging by the accounts in the papers.

I haven't received that ABC of L.M.S. railways that Mr Edgerton sent up for, so I suppose that, after 12 months, it has been forgotten. I will send up for it myself next vac.

Has the piano been tuned yet? I hope to do plenty practising in the holidays. Mummy must start playing again soon, then we can play as duets (?) (!)

Having spent nearly an hour writing this letter, I am suffering extreme (!) mental exhaustion, so I will conclude Volume 2 with thanks for the money and addresses, gratefully received.

Love from, Shirley

P.S. Bowyer,[125] a boy in our study had to go home with appendicitis, which he had out yesterday.

This doodle by Michael appeared at the end of his voluminous letter of the 10th December 1944.

---

[124] The Ellerton Prize (after E. Ellerton, Master 1798-1810) is awarded each year for the best performance by a chorister in school examinations.

[125] G.B.O. Bowyer had joined the Lower Fourth Form of MCS in September 1943.

Michael's reference in his letter of 10th December, above, to an explosion near Burton refers to the huge explosion that occurred at 11:11am on Monday 27th November 1944 at the RAF Fauld underground munitions storage depot. The explosion was one of the largest non-nuclear explosions in history and the largest to occur on UK soil. The exact death toll is uncertain, but it is believed that about 70 people died.

BOMB DUMP KILLED AND MISSING 68: Total of Missiles Destroyed Less Than 4,000 Tons. Sir Archibald Sinclair, Air Minister, making a statement in the Commons to day on the Burton-on-Trent munition explosion, said the total number of people killed and missing was 68. 'The total loss of bombs is less than 4,000 tons; no more than dropped in a single raid on Germany.' he said.
Oxford Mail, Thursday 30th November 1944

Each Christmas, as a chorister at MCS, Michael was required to stay-on in Oxford after the term had ended, to sing at the Magdalen College Christmas Services and other festivities. This meant that he would usually have travel back to his home in Stafford on Christmas Day, causing him much concern each year that, due to the restricted services on the Bank holiday, he may get stranded in Oxford. Announcements, like that shown below from the *Oxford Mail*, warned the general public not to expect a service at Christmas.

NO EXTRA TRAINS AT CHRISTMAS. *Oxford Mail*, Monday 22nd November 1943

Spring (Hilary) Term 1945

When Michael returned to Oxford on 10th January 1945, he was greeted with chilly weather that had persisted, producing frosty, icy conditions since the start of the year. Although the weather was to warm up in the middle part of January, the cold snap returned towards the end of the month to produce arctic conditions perfect for tobogganing.

Young Oxford skates, toboggans and slides on the ice at Jackdaw Lane,
Iffley Road, Oxford.
Oxford Mail, Wednesday 3rd January 1945

Oxford schoolboys tobogganing on the slopes at South Field Golf Course, Oxford.
Oxford Mail, Monday 29th January 1945

Boys were not permitted to have mains radios in their studies and electricity throughout the boarding house rooms was turned off during the day except for the library. To run a 'secret' study radio the boys ran a lead from a light on the stair into one study, then on from here out of a window and upstairs to a second study. The boys were eventually sure that Mr Elam knew of the wiring job and the radios, but 'he preferred a quiet life'. Michael recounted that the boarders loved listening to the Axis Propagandist Lord Haw-Haw, 'a source of

endless merriment' ... 'nobody believed a word he said and we used to fall about laughing'.

Monday Morning [15th January 1945]

Dear Mummy,

I am now safely installed back at school in the old study, and I have finished all my unpacking. Unfortunately, I don't know where those papers are; you can't imagine how sorry I am that such a thing could happen.

Have you looked in all my things and in the sideboard cupboard?

I am going to try to get you a print of Magdalen Tower for a birthday present, only I don't know how much they are.

We have got a wireless in our study now and can listen to whatever we want ('ITMA'[126] is very popular).

I suppose you've heard that Syd Walker[127] is dead; it's rather a pity as he was to have started a new programme this next week.

The concert of the three choirs is on Feb 15th and one of the big pieces is being conducted by the composer (Benjamin Britten) whose autograph I will try to get.

By the way, the boy who is taking my place in the play has got protruding teeth and no voice. I am annoyed!

Cairns was very thrilled with his present, which I gave him when I got back.

---

[126] 'ITMA' refers to the BBC radio comedy programme 'It's That Man Again', which ran from 1939 to 1949. The title refers to a contemporary phrase concerning the ever more frequent news stories about Hitler in the lead up to War. ITMA made a radio superstar of Tommy Handley and is believed to have played a major role in sustaining morale on the UK's 'home front' during War. It also popularised the catch phrases such as 'TTFN – Ta-Ta for now' and 'Can I do you now, Sir?'.
[127] Syd Walker was a British actor who died aged 58 on 13th January 1945.

On Tuesday I went to see those two funny men that I wanted to see on Sunday at the Odeon. They were in 'Lost in a Harem'[128] and it was very funny. I will write to you on Friday and address it to Christleton.[129]

Enjoy yourself there, from Shirley

LOST IN HAREM. The Oxford Times, Friday 5th January 1945

Wednesday [31st January 1945]

Dear Daddy,

Although you said in your letter 'Don't Write' I felt I must before you leave.

Last Friday we had a fire at school house. It demolished a large part of the roof of Mr. Stanier's house, but fortunately failed to damage our part of the house. The seniors of the house had to fight the blaze until the advent of the fire brigade, and I helped carry water. The fire lasted 3 hours, and at the end there were 3 fire escapes, several small fire-engines, two big ones, a searchlight and goodness knows what else. The weather was so cold that the water froze in a few moments; and they could not get water from the river as the ice was 4 inches thick.

---

128 *Lost in a Harem* was a film starring the comedy team of Bud Abbott and Lou Costello.
129 Christleton is a village on the outskirts of Chester where Michael's extended family lived.

No-body had to evacuate and we spent the time in the dining hall.

Yesterday the snow was 6 inches to a foot deep in Oxford and we had great fun, but now it has all gone and the floods are coming up.

What is the name of the Oxford 'tec' on your course? If I asked for him at Oxford station, do you think that he would get me in there to look around?

I hope that you have done well on your course and passed with flying colours.

Sorry for such a short letter,

From your loving son, Shirley

The *Oxford Mail* reported that the fire which broke out at the School threatened to spread over the entire roof. Serious damage, and perhaps loss of life was prevented by the efficient work of the boys' fire-fighting team fighting the blaze until the arrival of the Oxford section of the NFS,[130] who took three hours to deal with the blaze. Weather reports in the newspaper the following week show the extremely cold and frosty conditions that hindered the firemen fighting the fire. The fire was first discovered by the headmaster's wife, Mrs Stanier, who heard crackling in a bedroom in the attic and Michael remembered that it was eventually discerned that 'The cause of the fire was the ignition of clothes left to dry by the room's occupant, a housemaid.'

---

[130] The National Fire Service (NFS) was the single fire service created in Great Britain in 1941 by the amalgamation of the wartime national Auxiliary Fire Service (AFS) and the local authority fire brigades. It existed until 1948, when it was again split by the Fire Services Act 1947, with fire services reverting to local authority control.

FIRE AT OXFORD SCHOOL

Boys Attack Out-break With Stirrup Pumps

A FIRE which broke out at Magdalen College School, Oxford, last night, and threatened to spread over the roof of the entire school, was prevented from causing serious damage, and perhaps loss of life, by the efficient work of a boys' fire-fighting team and the Oxford section of the N.F.S., who dealt with the blaze in three hours.

A fire-fighting party of boys who board at the school were fighting the blaze until the arrival of the firemen.

The fire was first discovered by Mrs. Stanier, wife of the headmaster, Mr. R. S. Stanier, who heard crackling in a bedroom in the attic.

Mr. Stanier gave instructions to the fire team, who engaged the blaze with stirrup pumps and buckets of water. By the time it was discovered the fire was burning fiercely through the beams, roof and floorboards.

The N.F.S. was quickly on the spot and pumps were also called in Witney, Woodstock and Clifton Hampden to stand by.

While firemen were coping with the flames a salvage crew was spreading tarpaulin sheets over furniture and beds to save them from being damaged by water and smoke.

Actually there was surprisingly little damage to the building by water. Fire damage was done to a large part of the roof above the room and beams were burnt away.

Conditions on the roof were exceedingly difficult owing to frost, which quickly froze the water and ladders rapidly became icy.

Divisional Officer G. W. Underdown was in charge and the Fire Force Commander, Mr D. M. Taylor, was present.

FIRE AT OXFORD SCHOOL: Boys Attack Out-break With Stirrup Pumps. *Oxford Mail*, Saturday 27th January 1945

After the Blizzard – A scene in an Oxford street yesterday. *Oxford Mail*, Wednesday 31st January 1945

Sunday [11th February 1945]

Dear Mummy and Daddy,

There's quite a lot of news this week. I am getting very excited now, as this week the Stratford-on-Avon Shakespeare Festival Company are at the New Theatre for a whole week, and they are performing 'Othello', 'Twelfth Night', and 'The Merry Wives of Windsor'. I hope to see 'Twelfth Night' on Wednesday evening, as there is no chapel then, it being Ash Wednesday also, I will try to see 'Merry Wives of Windsor' on Saturday afternoon.

Yesterday the 1st XI (Hockey) beat Stowe School, 3-2, which is pretty good, as they were huge chaps.

This term I am in Number 3 platoon of the J.T.C., and next month I will be sitting for the Cert 'A' examination (Part I). If I pass this, I will take Part II, and if I pass that, I will be an N.C.O. (!) (Not that I will ever pass Part II!)

How is my bicycle getting on? I am looking forward very much to riding down the road on it.

It was a thrill when I heard that Daddy has passed his exams., but WHAT IS IT ALL IN AID OF? ARE WE LEAVING STAFFORD? ETC., ETC., ETC. ....

Also, How is Bim getting on? Tell her to be good, and perhaps soon she will lead the Larder Guard.

As our history is getting more and more interesting, I have taken the opportunity of buying 'A short history of the English People', by J.R. Greene,[131] and I haven't regretted the decision, although it cost me 6/-. Actually, up to now, I have been pretty careful with my money.

---

[131] John Richard Green (1837 - 1883) was himself expelled from MCS in 1854 for writing a very critical essay of Charles I. After serving as an Anglican curate, Green set out to write a history of the English nation. 'A short history of the English People' was a pioneering history text based on the people of England rather than its political leaders, governments, and battles. It became one of the most popular history books of the Victorian era and continued to sell in the succeeding decades.

Have you written to Mr. Stanier about my feet yet? I would like it very much if something could be done about them, as I cannot do anything in games like rugger, as I am much too slow; also, I don't stand a chance in the sports, and it embarrasses me when I come last in 'runs' etc.

So please try to do something about it.

That's about all, so goodbye, from Shirley

SHAKESPEARE FESTIVAL. *Oxford Mail*, Saturday 10th February 1945

In March and April 1945, the closing stages and the rapid progress of the war were reported by the *Oxford Mail* with compelling headlines, portraying the advances of the Allies and the joining up of the British and U.S. front from the West with the Soviet front from the East. The eventual collapse of Germany and the end of the war in Europe was

now in no doubt and planning for the Victory in Europe (VE) Day was much in evidence in the Oxford newspapers.

'MONTY' ACROSS RHINE: GOING WELL.
Oxford Mail, Saturday 24th March 1945

BRITISH – U.S. LINK-UP: RUHR CUT OFF.
Oxford Mail, Saturday 31st March 1945

SOVIET – U.S. LINK-UPS ON WIDE FRONT.
Oxford Mail, Saturday 28th April 1945

Oxford's 'V' Day Plans Take Shape: No Floodlighting – Later Possibility. The bells at Carfax and other central towers will be rung, beginning about one hour after the 'Cease Fire' has been ordered, and all ringers are asked to assemble at Carfax Tower within that time. *Oxford Mail*, Thursday 19th April 1945.

DRINK HOURS ON VE DAY: Oxford Extension to 11 o'clock. The Oxford Magistrates granted to-day an extension of licensed hours on VE Day from 10p.m. to 11 p.m. *Oxford Mail*, Friday 4th May 1945

Oxford University VE Day Holiday. It is announced that VE Day will be observed as a holiday at Oxford University. *Oxford Mail*, Friday 4th May 1945

Summer (Trinity) Term 1945

Sunday [29th April 1945]

Dear Mummy and Daddy,

The first letter home!! (Well, at least it's written on a Sunday)!

I hope you are both well; I am full of life and kicking out strongly and I have settled down again to school life. Our study is still the same, - same people etc., and the bottom passage has been redecorated.

The journey down to Oxford was foul. I stood in the corridor most of the way to Bletchley, as I couldn't bear these awful folk in my compartment. When I eventually arrived at Oxford it was 3 o'clock as I had missed my connection at Bletchley, where I waited till about 2 o'clock.

I think that now I am capable of keeping a fountain pen, could you please send it as soon as possible, and thank you very much!

I think I had better stop now as it is very warm out.

Goodbye from Shirley

On Monday 7th May came the announcement that Germany had signed a total and unconditional surrender, to be effective from the following day, Tuesday 8th May. 1945. The VE day celebrations that followed in Oxford were, to say the least, animated and spirited, but not unsurprising considering the release of tension after five long years of war.

GERMANY SURRENDERS: ALL FIGHTING CEASES IN EUROPE: VE DAY
STATEMENT THIS EVENING.
Oxford Mail, Monday 7th May 1945.

Oxford Mail, Tuesday 8th May 1945.

LIVELY SCENES AT OXFORD. VE Day celebrations livened up at Carfax this afternoon, when a large crowd – mostly of British Service men and boys – made it exceedingly dangerous for motorists to pass through; the Police advised motorists to take the side streets. Cars and vans were stopped and shaken from side to side, and one baker's van, which underwent the process had its doors torn open and loaves of bread spilled onto the pavement. Some loaves were thrown back into the van, but most of them went flying into the air. The bread was then continuously thrown about and buses were bombarded. A light army truck next received attention and the officer, who was sitting beside the driver, had his cap taken off by an airman, but after some persuasion it was returned. A bus containing American soldiers was cheered, but before it had ploughed its way through the mass of people one of its windows was smashed in. Luckily no-one was hurt.

Theft of Flags. Many flags in Queen Street, Oxford, were stolen last night and young hooligans were seen at Carfax carrying flags of which they had set the sticks alight. Mrs M.E.D. Earl; tobacconist, H.B. Tyler Ltd.; the City Treasurer's office, Arthur Bennett Ltd.; and the Maypole Dairy lost flags. Mr Joseph Colegrove of 226 Banbury Road, Oxford is offering a reward of £5 for information about the theft of flags festooned from tree to tree in his garden.

Bonfires of packing cases were made by a crowd of over 500 soldiers and civilians at Carfax last night. Traffic was stopped for free rides, mock political speeches were made, and there were dancing and singing.

Those Victory Smiles: G.I.s and Oxford postwomen
spread the glad news at Carfax.
Oxford Mail, Tuesday 8th May 1945.

OXFORD CARNIVAL SCENES: City and District Revelry for Two Days and Nights. Oxford and the District have had two phenomenal days and nights with the VE celebrations. In the City and its suburbs there were dozens of street tea parties yesterday for children. Last night and the night before floodlighting and in all the main thoroughfares as well as side streets bonfires were features of the celebrations.

Hundreds of people gathered round bonfires in Broad Walk, High-street and Carfax, and sang and danced on Tuesday night.

Oxford Mail, Thursday 10th May 1945.

About 20 exuberant youths pushed Oxford's oldest fire engine, a horsed drawn hand pump, from an open space adjoining the social centre in New Road, where it was kept to Carfax, where it was taken over by the crowd. Shop windows were broken in Walton Street and Queen Street.

DOUBLE CELEBRATION. There was a double celebration in Black Friars Road, St Ebbe's, on VE Day, where loudspeakers relayed dance music from a gramophone.

C.S.M Harold Hastings of No.7 returned from a German prison camp where he had been released after five years of captivity.

People carried him shoulder high.

Monday 14th May 1945

Dear Mummy and Daddy,

The first letter of peace!

And my goodness, did we celebrate VE-DAY!! When it was announced on Monday evening that VE-DAY would be Tuesday, we were all in prep., and people embraced each other, threw books around, hugged the prefect who was taking prep., and generally made a terrific noise. Then the whole lot of us rushed down on the field and made a huge bonfire. We baked potatoes on it and danced around it until 11.15pm. By this time Magdalen Tower was beautifully flood-lit. We were all singing and dancing on the 'Spit' and hundreds of Oxford people watched us from Magdalen Bridge. Eventually we crept off to bed at 11.30. On Tuesday we got up at 7 o'clock and sang in dorm until breakfast. Cairns took me out to lunch at his house; then the two of us went to the flicks and after that, out to tea at the house of some of Cairns friends. I had to leave there for chapel, but went back after evensong, and they had me there till 10 o'clock. We all walked back to school, and I went into dorm, where there were only six of us, as the others had all gone home. Somebody bought a small electric cooker into dorm, and it was plugged into a light. We were all enjoying sardines on toast and fried bread when Mr Elam and Mr Greenham walked in. They didn't mind at all, but brought us another loaf of bread and a big hunk of cheese. After this we listened to the midnight news and sang a bit. And so to bed.

The next day (Wednesday) was also a whole holiday. In the morning I went out with Cairns and we both had a lousy lunch at the 'Angel'. I went out to tea with the Cairns again for tea, with Saunders and Webb. There was no chapel, and we left Cairns house at 8 o'clock. Saunders and Webb had to go back to school, but Cairns and I had perm. to be out till 10.30, and we went up town to watch the celebrations in the city centre. The undergrads were madly racing around in big processions, throwing fireworks into huge crowds. Motor-cars were being turned over, and a baker's van was looted and the loaves used as ammunition for an inter college rag. Bonfires were lit in the middle of the streets by undergraduates who stopped traffic and kicked the sides of any buses or cars which happened to being going through. A jeep was completely dismantled by the crowd, but I didn't see that. At about 10 o'clock I was outside Magdalen College, where phosphorous was being thrown into the roads and burnt. Gramophone music was being played through loud speakers and <u>hundreds</u>, literally hundreds of people were dancing in the road. An American officer pulled a brand-new forage cap out of his pocket and gave it to me. We went back to school, but were allowed out till 11, and all the senior dorm. went out to enjoy the fun.[132] Unfortunately, I had to get up at 7 o'clock on Thursday for communion; school began again on Thursday.

Could you send all those drawings of mine which are in my Hornby Train drawer, <u>except the big ones</u>.

I was 20th in form.

Best wishes from Shirley

The Angel Restaurant that Michael dined at with Brian Cairns on the second day of the VE public holiday (Tuesday 8th and Wednesday 9th May 1945) was a popular and inexpensive, Oxford & District Co-operative society run restaurant on the High Street in Oxford. In total, Oxford had three 'special' public holidays to celebrate Victory in Europe, the third one being almost a month later, on Monday 4th June. During this period of excitement and celebration, Oxford was busy removing the accoutrements of a city during war and rapidly regaining its pre-war aesthetics.

---

[132] Michael's fellow ex-chorister friend Roger Firkins remembers 'the best bit for me was getting as much paper as possible from public loos and winding [it] round a bus in Cornmarket'.

OXFORD'S THIRD VE HOLIDAY, 4 JUNE.
Oxford Mail, Thursday 17th May 1945.

Another war link goes: Members of the Oxford N.F.S. removing surface pipes in High Street, Oxford. *Oxford Mail*, Friday 1st June 1945.

Autumn 1945 – Summer 1946

Hello Michael, Eights Week and V-Day Celebrations

When Michael returned to school in September 1945, Oxford, Britain and the whole world was rapidly changing, politically and socially. The *Oxford Mail* headlines at the time allow a peek at some of the events and transformations taking place during this historic period. In late July 1945 an unexpected landslide victory for Clement Attlee's Labour Party, over Winston Churchill's Conservatives was declared. The following week the United States dropped atomic bombs on the Japanese cities of Hiroshima and Nagasaki, finally prompting the Japanese government to surrender and effectively end the Second World War. Meanwhile in Britain, the Government seeing the importance of atomic research gave the go ahead to start work on an atomic research site at Harwell, 'the first in Europe', bringing with it many job opportunities to the Oxford area.

Oxford like most major towns across Britain saw the construction of prefabricated houses, a major part of the plan to address the post–Second World War housing shortage. These cheap, temporary houses were initially promised and announced by Winston Churchill in a broadcast in March 1944, and legally outlined in the Housing (Temporary Accommodation) Act of 1944. So successful were the 'Prefabs', like the temporary buildings at MCS built in 1928, many outlived their ten to forty-year life expectancy and some are still cherished homes today, like the BISF construction type in the Barton and Sandhills area to the east of Oxford.

OVERWHELMING LABOUR VICTORY. *Oxford Mail*, Thursday 26th July 1945

JAPAN FACES ALL – OUT ATOMIC BOMB ONSLAUGHT: HIROSHIMA ATTACK ONLY A WARNING. City Believed Wiped Out; Tokio May Be Hit Next. *Oxford Mail*, Tuesday 7th August 1945

JAPS ASK FOR PEACE. 'WILL ACCEPT POTSDAM ULTIMATUM': CONDITION SOUGHT. *Oxford Mail*, Thursday 10th August 1945

START ON HARWELL ATOM FACTORY THIS WEEK. Scientists, many of them from Oxford, are to get busy at once in a series of small sheds, and in light of their experience they will design and plan the lay-out of the huge range of buildings. *Oxford Mail*, Thursday 30th October 1945

Oxford's first prefabricated house going up at the Barton Estate, Headington. *Oxford Mail*, Wednesday 19th December 1945

'PREFAB' GOING UP AT OXFORD: Shell, Roof, Fittings All in Place Within Five Days. *Oxford Mail*, Wednesday 19th December 1945

Autumn (Michaelmas) Term 1945

For this academic year, in order to help him concentrate on his other subjects Michael was allowed to drop Greek. Discussions had taken place between his father and the Headmaster about Michael potentially studying History, his favourite subject, at university. He would be sitting his School Certificate exams in July 1946, and, if he was to stand any chance of eventually getting a History Scholarship he would first have to pass these successfully, and then embark on his Higher Certificate exams in 1947.[133] The headmaster, Mr Stanier, in a letter to Michael's father, stated in no uncertain terms that Michael must work much harder in his final years of his schooling.

---

[133] School Certificate examinations were usually taken at age sixteen and performance in each subject was graded as Fail, Pass, Credit or Distinction. Students had to gain six passes to obtain a certificate. To obtain a matriculation exemption for entry to university students usually had to obtain at least a Credit in five subjects including English, Mathematics, Science and a Language. Students who passed the School Certificate were able to stay on at school if they wished to take the Higher Certificate at age eighteen. The School Certificate and Higher Certificate were abolished on the introduction of GCE O-Level and A-Level examinations in 1951.

From THE MASTER,
Magdalen College School, Oxford.

Telephone: Oxford 2191.

28th November, 1945.

Dear ~~Mr.~~ Hickey,

Many thanks for your letter.

I am afraid I have slipped up over the new Regulation. At the moment it does not apply to Boarders. This seems very illogical and we are trying to get it altered. If we do I will send you the necessary forms.

I am sorry about your rheumatism and hope that things will soon be easier!

I have already allowed Shirley to drop Greek and I hope that this will have some effect on his other work, but I think I ought to give you fair warning that his view of his prospects in School Certificate is highly optimistic. He is definitely a weak candidate all round though History is his best subject. Even allowing for Choir duties he ought to be working more than

he is. The long and short of it is that though I should be delighted if he could get a History Scholarship he will have practically no chance of doing so unless he gets through the School Certificate next July and he will not get through the School Certificate unless he works much harder. I ~~will tell~~ him this myself and possibly you may feel like rubbing it in. I was talking about him to the President the other day and the President pleaded on his behalf that his voice breaking so late may be the cause of lack of energy etc. I think there is something in this but at the same time I think he ought to realise that he is asking for trouble if he thinks that on his present showing he will pass in everything except Greek and Maths.

Best wishes,

Yours sincerely,

have told !

Sunday [2nd December 1945]

Dear Mummy and Daddy,

There is rather a lot of news this week, and hope that this will be a long letter.

The head-line is rather surprising; Yesterday, Mr Taylor told me that I would be singing some solos in the Sheldonian Theatre to-day, in the big annual Carol Service. The choir is not singing, and I will be singing 'Good King Wenceslas' with some baritone, piano, organ, and orchestra. It ought to be rather fun, singing to 1,000 people.

The 'Messiah', last Sunday was terrific. All the trumpet bits were done by Jack Mackintosh[134], one of the best in England, and the soloists were famous too.

Yesterday, I played rugger, and converted a try, about the first I have ever done, and got two points for my side, (which lost anyway) (17-16) !

The 1st XV has won two more matches, and I think it will win every other match this term.[135]

I have already started to buy Xmas Cards, and I will start making my own soon.

I wonder if Mrs Lee still wants her gramophone ???? – (Hint!).

I got top marks in a big test on 'Macbeth' last Tuesday, and the master (the one we saw at Parkgate) was very pleased, and I had to read my paper out to the form.

I have written a letter to the Editor of the 'Lily' – (sorry, I told you that last week!)

---

[134] At that time Jack Mackintosh, 'The Cornet King', was playing for the BBC Symphony Orchestra.
[135] Indeed, the MCS 1st XV did win all thirteen of its matches played that term, notably beating its local rivals Abingdon 31-0.

'To-morrow the World'[136] is on at the new Theatre next week, with the complete cast from London, so I might go to see it, as it's said to be a very good play.

On the 16th of this month, we have the Carols in the Ante-Chapel. This is to warn you, in case Uncle Eric has some petrol.[137]

Well, in 23 days, I will be home, eating the jolly old Xmas pud, so prepare the fatted calf, etc. in eager anticipation.

Thank you very much for the 5/-.

From Shirley

This doodle by Michael appeared at the end of his 2nd December letter.

TO-MORROW THE WORLD. *The Oxford Times*, Friday 30th November 1945

---

[136] 'Tomorrow, the World' is a play about a young German boy (Skip Homeier) who had been in the Hitler youth before going to live with his uncle in the United States.
[137] Petrol rationing didn't end until May 1950.

Tuesday [11th December 1945]

Dear Mummy and Daddy,

Just a very short note to assure you that I am all right now, I have had a nasty chill, but no trace of a Bronchial cough. Exams start on Friday, so I am busy 'cramming'. I hope Bim is all right. I will be sending <u>her</u> a Christmas Card all to herself. Please send the address if poss. Likewise my bow-tie. I am going to make the best of this, my last, extra week.

Think of it, only three more weeks and then ... !

Well that's all for now.

From Shirley[138]

This doodle by Michael appeared at the end of his 11th December letter.

---

[138] This is the last time Michael signs his name as Shirley. All letters from this date onwards are signed 'Michael'.

Spring (Hilary) Term 1946

Skating and the return of the banana:

Skating on Port Meadow, Oxford – A scene yesterday afternoon.
Oxford Mail, Thursday 17 January 1946

BANANAS AT LAST: Picture taken at Messrs. Hicks and Son warehouse in Oxford to-day as the first bananas were received. *Oxford Mail*, Monday 29th January 1946.

Bananas on sale in Oxford to-day. Hundreds of stems of bananas have been ripening in Brewer and Tyrrell's heated cellars in the Market, Oxford, this week, and will be on sale in Oxford shops to-day. *Oxford Mail*, Saturday 2nd February 1946.

Sunday [February 1946]

Dear Mummy and Daddy,

What a dull week this has been! I have had very little spare time for anything, and no games either, as the weather is so damp; the river has begun to flood the field and the boating raft is under water.

The first XI hockey team is very good; they have had 3 matches against colleges, and won one of them 13-3, which was a great victory.

There is no debate tonight so I will read my history book. So far my lessons are going well, and I don't think I will be bottom this time.

The other day, I was in doors with a cold, but not in bed, so I started making one of those big flying model aeroplanes, like those you see at Commem. in the exhibition.

I have been to the Food Office about those extra clothing coupons, and they say I must take in my old book, so can you send it quickly?

The other day I wrote to Jean, and she says that I am welcome to stay with her next holidays, or even at half-term, if there is a holiday then. Next week, she is sending me a chocolate cake.

Yesterday, my French friend sent me a lovely bunch of magazines – war papers, post cards, and a lovely painting (by himself) of a little street.

Well, the post is about to go, so cheerio from Michael.

Spectator attendance at sports events immediately after the war significantly increased. Indeed, the popularity for rugby at the Iffley Road ground, especially when the visitors were an international team, was evident in the crowd size depicted in the *Oxford Mail* photo when New Zealand played the University team in February 1946.

SATURDAY, 16 FEBRUARY, 1946

THE SCHOOLBOYS SAT BY THEMSELVES

A scene at the Iffley-road ground, Oxford, on Thursday. Could these youngsters have learned more from the Kiwis' play? The Sports Editor discusses British methods of coaching in his weekly article.

THE SCHOOLBOYS SAT BY THEMSELVES. A [packed] scene at the Iffley-road ground, Oxford on Thursday [Oxford University 9 v New Zealand 31]. *Oxford Mail*, Saturday 16th February 1946

Sunday [24th February 1946]

Dear Mummy and Daddy,

This letter is rather late, and I hope that it will catch the post.

I wasn't able to put pen to paper this morning or this afternoon, as this morning I was playing hockey, and this afternoon, I went out rowing in a 'pair' with Saunders (although I am not in the rowing club), which we both enjoyed very much. It was the first time I had ever rowed on sliding seats, and we got up a good speed, and had races with some other chaps who were also in a 'pair' (a 'pair' is boat in which two people do the rowing, and one steers).

In a fortnight's time, I am going to have a crowded weekend. On Friday the 8th, I am taking the J.T.C. Certificate 'A' exam,[139] on Saturday there is a big dance here, which I might go to, if I learn enough steps, and on the Sunday, Canon Bisdee is taking me to a big concert in the Town Hall, the 'Requiem' by Brahms, and Gwen Catley[140] is singing in it. We are in the two best seats in the place, I believe, as he booked well in advance.

I mustn't forget to thank you for the lovely parcel, which came on Friday. Everything arrived in one piece, and I am going to write to Mrs. D. as soon as possible, also Aunty B. Last week I wrote to Daddy at Belson, and Jean.

I hope you didn't mind my getting those Wellingtons. They are a jolly good pair, but the price rather shook me – 29/-, but you can't get gum boots any cheaper nowadays.

Believe it or not, I am still keeping my diary!

A short time ago, I sent up to Jean Kent, a new British film-star, for her autograph, and I got back 6 photographs, all signed, and a letter, also signed. I am now a member of her 'International Fan Club', and every month I get a magazine, which is full of information about British Films.

On Saturday I went to see 'Perfect Strangers', with Robert Donat and Deborah Kerr.[141] It was a beautiful film, and I should see it if I were you.

Well goodbye now till next week.

From Michael

---

[139] Michael was awarded Cert A, Part I in the Hilary term of 1946, and Part II at the end of the Hilary term of 1947.

[140] Gwen Catley (1906 – 1996) was a famous English coloratura soprano renowned for the clarity and agility of her voice, who sang in opera, concert and revues.

[141] *Perfect Strangers* is a 1945 British film that saw the uncredited film debut of Roger Moore in a supporting role.

PERFECT STRANGERS. Oxford Mail,
Thursday 21st February 1946

Jean Kent International Fan Club
membership card and signed
photograph.

The Brahms Requiem referred to by Michael in his letter of 24th February was actually performed at the Sheldonian Theatre on Sunday 10th March and not at the Town Hall. It was part of the Oxford Bach Choir and Oxford Orchestral Society's memorial concert for Sir Hugh Allen, the influential British musician who, after being hit by a motorcycle near the Martyrs' Memorial, Oxford, had tragically died three days later on 20th February 1946, aged seventy-six, at the Radcliffe Infirmary. Michael had been lucky enough to meet Allen on at least two occasions, holding him in such high esteem that he collected his autograph when he had seen him in 1941.

Professor of Music Badly Hurt: Sir Hugh Allen in Oxford Accident.
Oxford Mail, Monday 18th February 1946

Oxford Memorial Concert.
Oxford Mail, Monday 11th March 1946

Sunday 3rd March [1946]

Dear Mummy and Daddy,

I was very surprised to hear about poor old Mrs. Lee; it must have been an awful shock for you to have found her, and I bet our Bim got a good shaken. She (Bim) only survived because coal gas, which is lighter than air, rose to the ceiling, and down on the floor, where Bim was, the air was relatively pure. Her next little kittens will be little gas-bags!

Yesterday, I went to see an old film called 'A Yank at Oxford' and it was very good indeed.[142] They had the singing on the Tower, but it wasn't done very accurately, as the 'choristers' weren't even singing the right

---

[142] *A Yank at Oxford* starred Vivien Leigh and Robert Taylor and was originally released in 1938. As a result of its success, a sequel (the 1942 film *A Yank at Eton*) and a parody (the 1940 Laurel and Hardy film *A Chump at Oxford*) were made.

thing! Still, it was very exciting and good, and Vivien Leigh acted very well.

On Thursday a lot of us went in the evening to see our school boxing team lose a match against the Y.M.C.A. and after the 'show', I got a lift back to school on a dayboy's motor-bike, it was great fun tearing down the High Street at 9.15 in the evening, and I enjoyed every minute of the 1½ miles back to school.

It has been snowing quite a bit this week, but not settled on the ground, thank goodness, although it has been quite cold.

We are all spending our free time learning our parts for the play, which is in about three weeks. Are you coming to it?

At the moment, we are all learning how to dance, as there is a Boat Club Dance on Saturday evening. I am wearing my best grey suit, so could you please send me my dog's head tie? (I won't get it dirty) Invitations have been sent to all the big girls' schools in the town, so that we won't be short of partners! As soon as I finish this letter, I will go downstairs and continue my dancing lessons, with the aid of a gramophone. I'll tell you all about the dance next week when I write and – PLEASE COULD YOU SEND ME SOME MONEY ??? (as I have spent 2/6 on a dance ticket!)

On Monday, the 1st XI (hockey) is playing a match against the University 2nd XI, the 'Occasionals', and after that, in about a week's time, the team of the English Hockey Association, almost the British International team.

I can hear the gramophone now, so goodbye from Michael

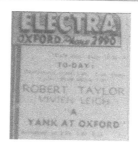

YANK AT OXFORD. *Oxford Mail*, Friday 1st March 1946

Sunday [10th March 1946]

Dear Mummy and Daddy,

I expect you are itching to know what I did at the dance last night, but before I tell you, I must thank you for the lovely parcel you sent me. It was grand to wear my dog's head tie again, and I'm sure that it created quite an impression.

Well, as you can imagine, there were quite a lot of us who couldn't dance very well, so we skipped the first few dances, as we could not pluck up enough courage to ask any of the girls to have a dance! Well, I was the first of the 'beginners' to ask for a dance; actually it was a Paul Jones,[143] so I was lucky. There were about one hundred boys and the same of girls, and it was fun! We did the Palais Glide, quicksteps, twosteps, waltzes, foxtrots, and before the last dance at 11, there was a terrific 'okie-kokey'[144] and we had two encores for it. Also, we did it the proper way, I'll show you next vac.

I was lucky enough in finding a partner. She was a month younger than I, and she wore a long light blue frock (Oh yes, half the girls, at least, wore long frocks). Well, it didn't take long to break the ice, and got to know each other so well that at the end of the dance, we kissed each other goodnight as I showed her to her taxi. Yes it certainly was a very good dance, and everyone enjoyed it.

As I write this letter, I have just coxed a four down the river to Iffley Lock. It was grand – the sun shone down, and we were almost the only boat on the calm river.

This afternoon, I am being taken by Canon Bisdee to a big concert in the Sheldonian and in which Gwen Catley is singing.

You will be pleased to know that I passed my J.T.C. Certificate 'A' on Friday; about 25 of us took it, and we all passed. I got 88 marks out of 100; the top boy got 95 marks, and the bottom 81. The commanding

---

[143] A 'Paul Jones' is a term for a social dance that involves changing partners, at a given signal, as an integral part of the dance.
[144] More commonly spelt 'hokey cokey' or 'okey cokey'.

officer [Captain C.B. Shepperd] and examiners all said that we were the best class for that exam in the history of the J.T.C. and that we were a credit to the school. Of course, we were horribly frightened when we had to stand in front of a fierce looking officer and answer his questions, and we were VERY GLAD when it was all over!! I am taking the second part of the exam in May, and if I get through that O.K. I will get my stripe.

I am enclosing an invitation to the play; just sign the dotted lines, and send the card marked X back to me. I would like you to come to the final performance on 23rd, if possible, as that is a Saturday, and in the afternoon we could go to the Theatre or somewhere. I think it will be very good, as we are rehearsing like mad.

If I want this letter to get to you tomorrow morning, I will have to post it now, so goodbye till next week from your loving son, Michael

---

The play Michael wanted his parents to attend on 23rd March 1946 was *Henry IV Part II*, in which Michael performed the part of Doll Tearsheet.

OXFORD BOYS IN *HENRY IV*.
Oxford Mail, Friday 22nd March 1946

Although the city of Oxford avoided any destruction by bombs during the war, much of the the Slade Army camp was destroyed by accidental fire in April 1946. The camp had been used for the reception of service men returning from overseas after the war and had only been closed down in the months previous to the fire. No military personnel were on duty at the time of the fire.

A scene at the Slade Camp, Oxford, last night, as the N.A.A.F.I., said to be one of the finest in the country, and the cinema were destroyed by fire.
Oxford Mail, Friday 5th April 1946.

Summer (Trinity) Term 1946

Sunday [May 1946]

Dear Mummy and Daddy,

Please excuse the writing, it is a new nib on my fountain pen, as the old one had started to throw blots.

I am working this morning, and this afternoon, I'm going to cycle to Dorchester,[145] where there is a big Roman Camp on a hill.

Now, for a great bit of news! Morley's mother says that certainly I can go to London for V-weekend, so please could you confirm it to? You see, Mr Stanier usually wants written permission for this sort of thing, so could you send me a letter as soon as possible saying yes? There is

---

[145] A twenty mile round journey.

a school holiday, so I won't be missing any work. I am looking forward to it ever so much. On Friday, Morley and I will travel to Guildford and spend the night at his house. Then, on Saturday, we will watch the procession from a good place, also we'll pop in to see Mr. Mckie. On the Sunday, we will spend the day in the country, on Monday we will go into London, see 'Caesar & Cleopatra' at the pictures and come back on an evening train.

I have got £1 put aside, so if you ask Mr. Stanier to have the return fare (17/-) on the bill. Otherwise, it won't cost much.

The other day I got three runs playing for the house at cricket.[146]

Yesterday, a junior with a fishing rod asked me to catch him a fish. So, not very hopefully, I put the line in, and caught a fish in about 15 seconds. It was about as big as the width of this page [4½ inches].

I did well in a French test the other day, coming 4th with 40 out of 50.

I have started the Mozart sonata, and I'm getting on quite well. The other day I played my Handel on the school organ, and it sounded rather good.

I haven't been to the pictures once yet this term; only to the theatre once. Next week I am probably going to see the International Ballet. Of course in the 1/6d seats every time!

Nothing else now, so goodbye from Michael.

P.S. Saunders wants to know when I'll be able to come in the summer vac., his mother says it's O.K.

P.P.S. Could you try and get some 127 films for me to take to London, please?

---

[146] Michael was in Wilkinson House, named after Frank Wilkinson who had died as a result of the First World War.

Sunday 26th May 1946

Dear Mummy and Daddy,

Thank you very much for the 4/6d, which will come in very useful; as you can guess, I'm counting the days till a week on Friday!

Incidentally, Mr Morley's address is:-

H. Morley, 'Symroyde', Silkmore Lane, West Horsley, Nr.Guildford, Surrey.

So if you want to write to him that's where to send it to.

'Eights week' started on Thursday, and I've been to see races every evening at 6.15. This is my first real eights week – all the barges have been done up for the occasion, and they are crammed with people.[147]

Some of us row down to the main river in a 'four' and watch from the bank. It is a terrific sight; hundreds of people rushing along the bank; the coaches signalling to their crews by firing blank ammunition from pistols, and all the lovely jackets and caps worn by rowing men. Magdalen are doing well, with a bump on every night except Friday. Last night they gave Christ Church a terrific bump, on the 'gut', nearly knocking the Christ Church cox in. On Thursday, Magdalen bumped Balliol so hard that the front part of their bow came off in Balliol's stern. Magdalen are now 4th, with every chance of becoming head of the river.

---

[147] No Eights week races were held in Oxford during the war years, so the 1946 event was indeed Michael's first experience of Oxford's Eights week.

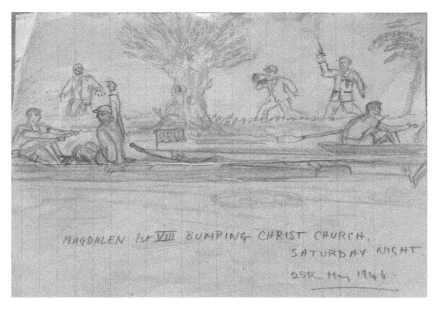

Pencil drawing by Michael, recording Magdalen's 'terrific' bump on Christ Church (at the 'gut' of the Isis River) that nearly knocked the Christ Church cox out of his boat.

We are doing plenty of revision work for School Cert. now. One of my weakest subjects is Chemistry, and I am working hard in that.[148]

At the piano, I am making good progress with the first movement of the Mozart sonata, which is stiff going.

I'll have to knock off now, so goodbye from Michael

---

[148] Michael's Chemistry teacher at this time was Captain Simmonds, 'Flick', who had return to the school in 1945 after serving in the Army.

'Gunmen' supporters at Oxford University Eights, which opened on the Isis yesterday. *Oxford Mail*, Friday 24th May 1946

The First Division race in progress last night at Oxford Eights May Eights, which concludes to-night. The Trinity Eight is still at the Head. *Oxford Mail*, Wednesday 29th May 1946

V.C. strokes Head of the River crew: R. Wakeford, who as a major won the V.C., is stroke of the Trinity Eight in Oxford May Eights.. *Oxford Mail*, Wednesday 29th May 1946

Oxford Mail, Thursday 30th May 1946

Sunday 2nd June 1946

Dear Mummy and Daddy,

It has been raining on and off here for about three days, and every time we go out rowing it comes down in buckets.

Eights week ended on Wednesday evening, and I saw every race; it was very exciting; Magdalen were 8th at the beginning of the week, but were 3rd at the end. Trinity were head of the river, Oriel second, Magdalen third.[149] After the last race the crews threw their coxes in, then jumped into the water themselves. The towpath was crammed tight with all sorts of people, mainly undergrads. and their girl friends. Everyone got frightfully excited when there was a bump; people fired guns into the air all the time. At the end all the eights went in a procession down the river; every one on the towpath and the barges cheered like mad. I wish you could have seen it.

Yesterday, we went out for the first time in our racing boat. As it was our first outing in a 'light' boat we weren't very good at first, but on the way back it was much better. We are racing against a Masters' IV soon; I think we ought to win.

I haven't been to the pictures yet this term. Once you get out of the cinema habit, you don't ever want to go to the flicks.

As you can guess, I'm looking forward like anything to next weekend.

My next letter may be written from Morley's home, but if my next letter is late, you'll know that I'll write on Tuesday for certain to tell you all about it.

The photo which I enclose was taken by Canon Bisdee outside his vicarage last term.

Have you been able to procure any films yet? If so, please send them so that they reach me on Thursday. The type is '127'.

Goodbye for now, from Michael.

---

[149] Trinity College had been 'Head Boat' in 1939.

Tuesday [11th June 1946]

Dear Mummy and Daddy,

I'm sorry I didn't write on Sunday, but I think you will forgive me as I was enjoying every minute of my stay at Morley's and in any case there wasn't enough time.

I'll start my account of the weekend from Friday, when we journeyed down to London on the 2.5[150] train jammed like sardines, although we all had seats. In our little party Platts and I were both going with Morley, Cairns and Lewi were going to Lewi's home, and two or three day boys made up the party. When we got to Paddington, we went to Waterloo by tube, (my first journey in one) breaking our journey at Piccadilly to see a few of the decorations. Once at Waterloo, we got onto an electric train which took us for 20 odd miles to Horsley. After a 2-miles' walk across the fields we got to Morley's house, which is with a few other houses right out in the beautiful countryside. After tea, we played bowls, then had supper and so to bed early at 9.30.

On Saturday we got up and had breakfast at 5.30, and got the first train into London, which was jammed tight. However, by 7.45 we were fairly near the front of a huge crowd by the entrance to Hyde Park opposite to St. George's Hospital[151]. Jammed tight we waited ...[152]

Then the Royal Family came by; we had a fine view of them, as they were only 20 yards away. The Queen was wearing a most extraordinary pale mauve hat just like a tea cosy. The whole family appeared to be

---

[150] It is assumed that the departure station was Oxford, but it is unclear what departure time 2.5 refers to.

[151] St George's Hospital at Hyde Park Corner closed in 1980, having relocated to Tooting. The old hospital building is now The Lanesborough Hotel.

[152] The date was Saturday 8 June 1946, and Michael and his friend were waiting to watch the London Victory Celebrations, a British Commonwealth, Empire and Allied victory celebration that consisted mainly of a military parade through the city and a night time fireworks display. Most British allies took part in the parade, including Belgium, Brazil, China, Czechoslovakia, France, Greece, Holland, Luxembourg and the United States. The parade arrangements caused a controversy surrounding the lack of representation of Polish forces.

wearing makeup. The King in admiral's uniform waved, the Queen smiled graciously, Princess Elizabeth smiled a bit, and Margaret Rose beamed all over her face. They were a fine sight in their landau, with uniformed attendants and a captain's guard of the Household Cavalry. Then we waited for another two hours. Suddenly we got free of the crowd and got up onto the masonry surrounded the gates of the park. There, our view was fine. The mechanised columns went a hundred yards from us, but the foot column, much better than the lorries and things split into two and came either side of us joining up when it was through the arch. We were about 3 yards from everything, and were right under the fly past, which dipped in salute. The planes were a terrific sight, flying wing to wing like this:

I thought that some were going to crash.

It took nearly 2 <u>Hours</u> for the procession of 21,000 men and women to get by us, and for 2 hours we stood on a little ledge between two pillars like this:

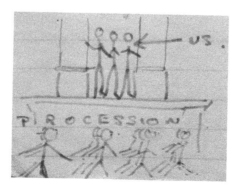

It was a grand sight, all the millions of people and thousands of soldiers, sailors and airmen who marched by twelve and sixteen abreast with dozens of bands, and all their battle honours. Every country of the Empire and the United Nations had sent its troops and civilians. The Greeks especially in their white skirts, looked wonderful.

At about 2.30, when the parade [ended], it started to rain, and, after meeting a dayboy friend we bolted into the biggest cinema in Europe, the 'Empire' Leicester Square, where we saw a not-very-thrilling film called 'Meet the Navy'.

It was still raining when, at 5 o'clock, we went to Waterloo to meet Morley's Aunt who was to be our guide for the evening. She had our macs, also our tea, which we ate on a luggage trolley. After this we walked across to Westminster Abbey. We didn't see Dr Mckie, but some other famous organist was playing the Coronation march 'Crown Imperial' by William Walton. It was most impressive. I saw the graves of Shakespeare, Handel, Pitt, Purcell, Gladstone, Disraeli and all the host of great men buried in the Abbey. Three quarters of an hour was not enough to see what I wanted to see, and I <u>must</u> go there again soon.

We wandered around then for a bit. Then at about 7.15, we managed to get into the third row of the crowd which was gathering at Westminster Bridge. We waited until 10 o'clock, but it wasn't boring, as all the boats were going back and to. Also a large fat woman was pushing her way through the crowd near us, so a man stuck his tie-pin into her behind! My, what a row!!!

Anyway, at 9.45, the King went under the bridge on his way down stream, to a salute of cheers, and all the ships down the river hooted.

On the dot of 10, he came back, and, at the moment when he set foot on the steps 300 yards away, dozens of searchlights went on all over London. They made a huge arch over the Houses of Parliament. Then the royal salute of forty one maroons went off; the whole crowd sang the National Anthem, and the Union Jack on top of Parliament was replaced by a floodlit Royal Standard. Suddenly, all the fire barges moored on either side of Westminster Bridge started off dozens of jets, which were lit by multi-coloured floodlights. It was beautiful to watch. Then, all the fireworks went off. I just can't explain what a tremendous sight they made. Every imaginable type of rocket went shooting up for nearly three hours. While the fireworks were on, we made our way down the Embankment (about a million other people had the same idea) and through floodlit Whitehall, but could not reach Trafalgar Square, where Nelson was floodlit on top of his column. The hundreds of loudspeakers were playing Handel's 'Fireworks Music', the 'Trumpet Voluntary', 'Pomp and Circumstance' by Elgar, and 'Crown Imperial', and many people seemed very moved. We got back to the Embankment via Scotland Yard, and after about an hour, got back onto Waterloo Bridge and thus to Waterloo Station and home. It was 2.30am. when I got to bed, and dawn was breaking; the birds were starting to sing. It had been a wonderful day, such as I will never forget, and I slept till 10.45 on Sunday morning.

On Sunday afternoon, Morley's cousin, (who is a detective sergeant) took us for a lovely ride all round that part of Surrey, which is the most beautiful county I've ever been in, with great hills and wooded valleys.

We played Monopoly on Sunday evening, and went to bed early.

On Monday we were up at 9 o'clock and took a walk down the pretty little village; then, after lunch, we went into town. There, we went to the 'Odeon' Marble Arch,[153] where we saw 'Caesar and Cleopatra' from the cheapest (4/6 !) seats. I am very glad that I have seen it, as it [was] magnificently staged, in Technicolour, Daddy would like it, I think, but Mummy would think probably rather like 'Henry V'.

I'm going to book 4/6 seats for Mummy and I on Commem. Saturday. I believe that the play is 'No Medals' which has just finished a long run in London.

I've got 'writer's cramp' now, so, hoping that you've enjoyed the letter, goodbye from Michael.

---

[153] In early 1945 the then Regal Cinema at Marble Arch was damaged by one of the last V1 flying bombs to hit London. It remained closed until September 1945, when it was re-opened by Odeon Cinemas as the Odeon Marble Arch.

NO MEDALS. *The Oxford Times*, Friday 21st June 1946

Whilst there were celebrations in London, Oxford had decided not to hold anymore victory celebrations as it attempted to return to normality with the removal of the public air-raid shelters and other war paraphernalia from around the city.

VICTORY DAY: THE CONQUERERS MARCH
Oxford Mail, Saturday 8th June 1946.

V-Day celebrations. — A view of the large crowd that had gathered in Trafalgar Square by 6 a.m. to-day.

The Royal procession passing through Admiralty Arch on its way to the saluting base in the Mall on Saturday.

No Oxford Victory Celebrations. Oxford City Council decided not to have any official victory celebrations, except for children. *Oxford Mail*, Monday 18th March 1946

Demolition of the air-raid shelter at the base of Carfax Tower, Oxford. *Oxford Mail*, Friday 14th June 1946

Friday [28th June 1946]

Dear Mummy and Daddy,

I've at last got time to write a longer letter than my earlier one this week, and I would like to tell you about the Stratford trip [Monday 24th June], which was what I call a good 'night out'. We left Oxford in a luxury coach at 5 o'clock, and with a master in the front seat. The journey there was beautiful, through wonderful countryside, and when we got to Stratford, we had almost an hour before the show began at 7.30. So we split up into parties, and our group visited Shakespeare's birthplace, the church where the immortal bard was christened and buried, a pub which sold 'Shakespeare Ales'. After this refreshment, we got into the theatre without further mishap, and it was a fine production. Then came the interval. There is a fine bar at that theatre .... .

Well, we saw the last part of the play and went back to the bus. It was getting dark, and in the back seats bottles of beer had appeared. We sang, someone was debagged (NOT I !) and his trousers were passed round the bus. It WAS fun, just like one of our Chippy outings in Beaty only with thirty seven people crammed into a bus meant for 27!! We got back at 12.30, and we all voted it a good night. Also, besides having a good time, we learnt a great deal about the play which did me well yesterday.

Love from Michael

Thursday [4ᵗʰ July 1946]

Dear Mummy and Daddy,

Thank you very much for the wonderful parcel, which was one of the best I've ever had from you, also I thank you very much for the money, which enabled me to have quite an enjoyable weekend.

I'm sorry that I haven't written earlier in the week, but all of us are swotting up like mad for School Cert. which starts, for us, on Tuesday. For my own part, I am confident of getting through. I have got six subjects in which I can pass; here is my forcast [sp. Forecast].[154]

English literature: Credit or Distinction

English language: Credit

English History: Credit or Distinction

Art: Credit

Latin: Pass

French: Pass

If that comes off (as I think it will) my Cert. will be a very good one, and not far short of a Matriculation.

---

[154] Michael's predictions were very accurate, for his 'School Certificate' he achieved the following standards in his six subjects (pass, credit, very good): English Language, Credit; English Literature, Credit; History, Very Good; Latin, Pass; French, Pass; Art, Credit;

On Sport's day,[155] Sir Henry Tizard came up to me and said that he'd heard that I was doing very well with my history, and that he would like me to try for a history scholarship to Magdalen.

If I can have the chance, I would like to take Higher Cert. next summer. Only three subjects need to be taken. I will probably take History and English as my main two subjects and Latin as my subsidiary subject.

I hope that my tonsils won't have to be taken out until a week after School Cert. as we have the 'Scratch fours' rowing races, and I am stroking a boarder 'A' crew. I will miss those if I go to hospital straight after School Cert.

I hope that you'll be able to come down to see either the races or my hospital ward.

Goodbye for now, from Michael

---

[155] After almost continuous rain for many days, the weather for the Sports days, Thursday 20th and Saturday 22nd June 1946, was fine.

Autumn 1946 – Summer 1947

A Royal Visit, Arctic Weather and Highers

Having turned seventeen in September 1946, Michael entered his final year of school as a confident young man starting to form his own opinion on politics and national affairs, enjoying the challenges of the cadet corps and becoming more engaged in rowing. He was almost unrecognisable from the young Shirley who had started at MCS seven years previous. For the Higher Certificate, which usually involved two years of study and be taken at the age of eighteen, Michael choose to study English and History as his 'Group II' subjects and Drawing as his subsidiary subject. To accomplish this in one year was going to require Michael to heed the warnings of his headmaster to work harder and stay focused.

Autumn (Michaelmas) Term 1946

Friday 18th October [1946]

Dear Daddy,

Many happy returns for today or tomorrow (I'm not quite sure when your birthday is)!

I was extremely sorry to hear of Insp. Weaver's death, he will be a great loss to Ryton.[156]

Last night I went to a debate at the Oxford Union, which I enjoyed very much. The motion was: 'This house applauds the domestic policy of the present Government'. The main speaker for the motion was Dr. Edith Summerskill[157] M.P. and the leading orator for the opposition

---

[156] Inspector James Weaver (a drill instructor at the training centre, Ryton on Dunsmore) died on 10 October 1946, aged 50, after collapsing while on duty.

[157] Edith Clara Summerskill, eventually Baroness Summerskill CH PC, (1901 – 1980) was a physician, feminist, Labour politician and writer. She was one of the first few women to be admitted to medical school and was one of the founders of the Socialist Health Association which spearheaded the National Health Service (1948). In 1938 she had initiated the Married Women's Association to promote equality in marriage and became its first president. During the War she had pressed for equal rights for women in the British Home Guard.

was Mr. John Boyd-Carpenter,[158] quite an intelligent Tory, with a great gift of sarcasm. Dr. Summerskill was extremely sincere, and placed her case far more plainly than any of the other speakers. She was assisted by a Labour M.P. for Portsmouth who also spoke extremely well. In my opinion, the Tory Party has had it if its bosses – Amery and Co. are big business men.

The Labour people certainly impressed me very much last night, and any Tory inclinations I ever had have been dispelled.

I am looking forward to coming home at half term, and Andrew and I will probably be coming by G.W.R., as the L.M.R. or the buses don't run at convenient times. Also, could you please send a line to Mr. Stanier giving written perm. for Andrew and myself to come home.

The end of this letter is lost

DR. SUMMERSKILL AT OXFORD UNION: Labour Policy Represented as Preventative Medicine.
Oxford Mail, Friday 18th October 1946

---

[158] John Boyd-Carpenter, eventually Baron Boyd-Carpenter, PC (1908 –1998) had recently become the Conservative Member of Parliament for Kingston-upon-Thames. He had studied History at Balliol College where he had been President of the Oxford Union in 1930.

Saturday Night [Michaelmas 1946]

Dear Mummy and Daddy,

Thank you for sending the keys – I certainly had forgotten clean about them. Before I forget, could you send my report (or is it already in my play box?).

As you can guess, I had a wonderful time at Shaw's. On the train down, I had a very good lunch, which included fried trout. When I arrived (I soon found the house) we all had coffee, then Uncle Frank took me to the news cinema, and showed me round a bit. After early dinner (cold roast Turkey!) Uncle Frank and I went to the Victoria Palace to see Lupino Lane[159] in a rather poor show, but we were in the 5th row of the stalls, and the music was rather nice.[160] We came back to sandwiches and I went to bed.

On Wednesday morning after a lovely breakfast of bacon and eggs, Uncle Frank took me round London on a bus. We saw all the bomb damage in the City, St. Pauls, Pic[c]adilly, Oxford Street, in fact all that matters, from the front seat upstairs in a London bus!

We went back to a lunch of beautiful liver. (The food there is just fine). With every meal (except tea + breakfast) I had lager beer, and before dinner I was given iced gin and grape fruit. (Mighty fine). After lunch I said goodbye, and to my surprise Uncle Frank gave me a pound! By myself I went to the Abbey by bus and met Dr. Mckie, who was very pleased to see me. He took me into the organ – and it's Terrific! After the service he played Handel's Overture to the Royal Fireworks Music which finishes on full organ and starts with trumpets. Then I met Canon

---

[159] Lupino Lane (1892 – 1959) was an actor and theatre manager, who appeared in a wide range of theatrical, music hall and film performances. He is best known for playing Bill Snibson in the play and film *Me and My Girl*, which popularised The Lambeth Walk.

[160] The show was *Sweetheart Mine*, written, produced, directed and acted in by Lupino Lane.

Adam Fox[161], who hasn't changed one bit since he left Magdalen. We had a good tea with some wonderful rich Australian Christmas cake, and then Dr. Mckie took me right round the Abbey, and I saw all the King's tombs, and the Coronation throne. I caught the 6.5p.m.[162] train from Paddington and got back at about 9. What a super time I'd had!

And one very important thing – I almost forgot! –

MANY HAPPY RETURNS

!!!!!!!?

With the £1 that Uncle Frank gave me I bought 4 records which I know you'll like, as they're all nice and quiet but very beautiful; they are:-

Bach's '2nd Brandenburg Concerto' (- 2 records)

Delius' 'La Calinda' and

Corelli's Oboe Concerto

I have just been playing them, and everybody likes them very much.

It's very foggy here at the moment, but not very cold.

Goodbye till next week from Michael

P.S. My big coat is admired by all.

Saturday Afternoon [26th October 1946]

Dear Mummy and Daddy,

I expect you're itching to hear about the royal visit, and as I got a fine view of everything, I'll tell you about it. For the whole week up to

---

[161] Adam Fox (1883 – 1977) had been the Dean of Divinity at Magdalen College until December 1941 and was one of the first members of the 'Inklings', a literary group which also included C.S. Lewis and J.R.R. Tolkien. Between 1938 and 1942 he had also been Professor of Poetry. He then became Canon of Westminster Abbey and later the Warden (Headmaster) of Radley College, before returning to live at a grace and favour apartment at Westminster's Little Cloister. Michael continued to pay him visits there until 1973, sharing a half bottle of Champagne and eating cake at each visit. He is buried in Poets' Corner at Westminster Abbey.

[162] It is unclear what departure time 6.5p.m. refers to.

Thursday we polished, pressed and cleaned up our J.T.C. uniforms, and when we paraded on Thursday morning we looked really smart. The King came from the station in a great big car with the Queen at his side, driving very slowly down the centre of the High Street. I was lining the route by St Mary's Church, and I saw them at a very short distance. After lunch, we went to Radcliffe Square and lined the King's path as he walked to the Bodleian. I was lining some steps directly opposite to the great library, and the King and Queen stopped to acknowledge the cheering less than three yards from me! I am in several news reels, I believe, as a cameraman 'got me in' with the Queen.[163] Then they walked slowly by, over to the door. The King tried to open it with a big silver key, but that broke, and after some delay, the door was opened from inside.

Next, we held back the crowds by the royal car as the King and Queen got in, and again, I could have tripped them up. I was touching the back of the car, about 3 feet from the King and Queen. (They were sitting in the open). It was really unforgettable; I would have loved you to have seen it. The King wore a terrific naval uniform, the Queen wore dove-grey with a feathery hat, and I thought she was very beautiful; also she isn't nearly as fat as the photographs make out.

Yesterday we had a field-day,[164] which succeeded in messing up our nice clean uniforms. I nearly caught a rabbit, but it got away.

I have got permission from Mr. Stanier to bring Andrew home next week-end, and we'll arrive home some time on Friday towards tea-time.

Till then, goodbye, and love from Michael

On Thursday 24th October 1946, King George VI and Queen Elizabeth visited Oxford to officially open the new building of the Bodleian Library. A special peal was rung on the bells of All Saints Church (now Lincoln College Library) to commemorate the event.

---

[163] The Junior Training Corps is seen helping to hold back the crowd as the King and Queen depart from the Bodleian in their car on British Pathé Archive Film ID: 2359.10; Media URN: 66358; between 4min 28sec and 4min 36sec.

[164] This field day was conducted somewhere in the Rousham Gap.

OXFORD WELCOMES KING AND QUEEN: BIG CROWDS – CHEERS – DECORATED STREETS. Station Ceremony Before Drive to All Souls Reception and Lunch.
Oxford Mail, Thursday 24th October 1946

The procession from the Clarendon Building across Broad Street to the New Bodleian Library, Oxford, during the visit of the King and Queen yesterday.
Oxford Mail, Thursday 24th October 1946

The scene as the King and Queen left the Sheldonian Theatre in procession for the new Bodleian Library for the opening ceremony.
Oxford Mail, Thursday 24th October 1946

COUN. W.C. WALKER (managing director of Benfield & Loxley, general contractors for the building of the New Bodleian) talking to the Queen after being presented to their Majesties at the opening ceremony yesterday. On left, next to the King, is the architect, Sir Giles Scott.
Oxford Mail, Thursday 24th October 1946

Spring (Hilary) Term 1947

The Spring term of 1947 was to bring a series of weather conditions that were to test the country to its maximum. After extreme cold in December, January brought snow and resultant electricity cuts across much of Britain. A sub-zero Fahrenheit temperature (-3F, -19 °C) was recorded in Oxford on 28th January 1947, the coldest it had been in the city since 1917. Michael later remembered it as 'the most savage winter of the century', recalling inkwells on the desks freezing and masters and pupils alike wore overcoats in class.

FIVE OXFORD SCHOOLS CLOSED THROUGH FROST.
Oxford Mail, Wednesday 29th January, 1947

Corporation workmen endeavouring to clear the frozen snow to-day from Oxford's pavements – where spills are numerous. *Oxford Mail*, Wednesday 29th January, 1947

ELECTRICTY POSITION GRIM - OFFICIAL.
Oxford Mail, Thursday 30th January, 1947

A picture taken to-day of the frozen river at Osney Bridge, Oxford. *Oxford Mail*, Thursday 30th January, 1947

FUEL POSITION DESPERATE: Power Cuts Throughout Snow-Bound Britain. *Oxford Mail*, Wednesday 5th February, 1947

Slow, but sure: Coal on the way to some Oxford homes, via St Aldate's. *Oxford Mail*, Thursday 6th February, 1947

20 Ft. Snowdrifts in N. Oxon. *Oxford Mail*, Thursday 6th February, 1947

Sunday [9th] February 1947

Dear Mummy and Daddy,

We've got six inches of snow here this morning, but it's not much good for snowballing, so I'm staying in. Yesterday went rowing, and I was very warm all the time, although ice had formed on the oars by the time we got back. I'm almost definitely going to be in the 2nd IV now, and I'll probably be stroke, which is the most important position in the boat. We have a race in about three weeks' time against the Old Boys' crew, and we start training tomorrow.

What do you think about the new school note paper? It was my idea to have it in double sheets.

Do you think you could let me have permission to have the cost of a concert to go on the bill? It is at the end of this month, and it is given in the Town Hall by the Boyd Neel Orchestra[165]; they are doing Bach's Brandenburg Concerto, and I would love to go. I don't want to break into my £1 note which is sealed up in an envelope but if you like I'll use it. (Still, I'd rather have it on the bill, as I'll want the £1 for our Boating dinner at the end of term, when we go to dinner at the George and the theatre)

Mr. Stanier thinks I am staying on after July to take a history Scholarship in December; he says that you wrote to tell him that it doesn't matter to you when I leave – I'm rather in the dark about it all, and I wish you'd clear me up about it.

Isn't the country in a wonderful mess? There are rumours of the Conservatives plotting to overthrow the present government and form a coalition – if that happens, we'll probably be out of the frying-pan into the fire!

I see that Coventry and Stafford were cut off for power the other day – I shouldn't think it's much of a joke for people with all–electric houses, but I think we at school are rather looking forward to another one – the first one we had came in the middle of school prayers and someone had to pump the organ!

I hope your back soon recovers – it's best to stay in bed nowadays!

Goodbye and love from Michael

The winter of 1946–47 was one of the harshest winters on record with the UK experiencing several cold spells, the coldest beginning on 21st January 1947. Large snow drifts blocked roads and railways, and coal supplies, already low following the War, struggled to get through to power stations resulting in many stations having to shut down due to lack of fuel. The government introduced several measures to cut power consumption, including restricting domestic

---

[165] Louis Boyd Neel (1905–81) was an English conductor and music academic (as well as a physician), best known for revitalising the genre of the chamber orchestra.

electricity to 19 hours per day and cutting industrial supplies completely. In addition, radio broadcasts were limited, television services were suspended, some magazines were ordered to stop being published and newspapers were cut in size. These measures badly affected public morale and turned the Minister of Fuel and Power, Emanuel Shinwell, into a scapegoat; he received death threats and had to be placed under police guard. Towards the end of February there were also fears of a food shortage as supplies were cut off and vegetables froze in the ground.

Light traffic was to be seen at the Plain, yesterday, after yet another fall of snow. [The MCS School House, in which Michael was boarding can be seen on the left.] *Oxford Mail*, Friday 7th February 1947

OXFORD USES CANDLES, OIL LAMPS, - AND MUCH MORE GAS.
Oxford is Responding Faithfully.
Oxford Mail, Thursday 13th February 1947

Road ovens in use to bake ice off the Oxford streets to-day. *Oxford Mail*, Wednesday 12th February 1947

Oxford Success of Boyd Neel Orchestra. *Oxford Mail*, Thursday 27th February 1947

Saturday evening [15th February 1947]

Dear Mummy and Daddy

It was lovely to get your wonderful parcel today – I don't think you've ever got so much into one packet! It will take me a good long time to get through it. (The cake is very good – how does it work?)

I've got the clothing coupons now, and (do you mind?) I took two of them for my colours cap and tie (I am stroke of the 2nd IV and will have my half-colours in 3 weeks) – I'll send the coupons as soon as possible.

As I was saying, I am now stroke of the 2nd IV and we have got 3 races coming off. The first one is Sat. March 1st, the second one (against Abingdon, the one you saw 4 years ago) on March 8th, and another about a week after. I have been told by the Vice-captain of Rowing that next term I'll probably be in the 'Summer 1st IV' which goes to Marlowe and Stratford regattas. My colours cap will have a long peak, like a cricket cap, and a red lily instead of white. The colours tie has equal red and black stripes about this wide

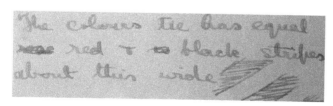

and looks lovely and gaudy. Next week are the 'Varsity Torpids' races, and this afternoon when we went on a practice row there were dozens of 'eights' on the river. The Oxford crew is already training at Henley, so we don't see them. The snow thawed a bit during the week, but the slush has now frozen solid and it's just horrible.

The boy who had meningitis died on Saturday, and everyone is very sorry, as he was a nice, quiet sort of chap.[166] There is no risk of

---

[166] Michael John Lardner came to MCS in September 1942. He actually died on Wednesday 12th February 1947, aged 16. He received prizes in Drawing and Singing while at MCS, had been confirmed by the Bishop of Oxford on 17th March 1945 and was the Organist in the School Chapel.

infection now, so don't worry. Anyway, you can't very well catch it unless you are very feeble (also, he was a dayboy, which renders the risk of infection practically nil).

I must close now, as 'dorm' has just been called and 'so to bed'.

Love from Michael

Dick Talboys, the Oxford University Boatman, fixing an ice-breaker to the bow of the University boat, to combat floating ice. *Oxford Mail*, Tuesday 4th February 1947

.... activity goes on as usual on the Isis as preparation for next week's Torpids reaches its climax. *Oxford Mail*, Saturday 15th February 1947

Preparing for next week's Torpid races at Oxford. *Oxford Mail*, Saturday 15th February 1947

An igloo built by the boys on Magdalen College cricket ground. *Oxford Mail*, Monday 24th February 1947

Saturday night March 1st 1947

Dear Mummy and Daddy,

We had our race postponed from today till next Wednesday because of the ice on the river and the bumping races which are being rowed on the Isis this week. We had a practice row this afternoon, the first for over a week, and several crabs[167] were caught; still, we have got a few days to go before the race and practice makes perfect.

You got me wrong, I think, about staying on at Oxford for the Boat race. The first I knew about it was when the boy asked me – it is apparently the parents' idea. I am spending the day there tomorrow, the fourth Sunday I have been there this term.

We are having a mock Higher Cert. exam soon, and I'm busy revising my History and English.

The other day I completed my 80th page of History essays!

On Friday I have a big J.T.C. exam – Certificate 'A', part 2; if we pass it we get a stripe, but as my work gives me little time for J.T.C. swotting, I don't expect I'll pass. Still, it doesn't worry me at all – I'd rather get Higher Cert. than be a corporal!

Is there still any snow at Stafford? It's nearly all gone from here, but it is still freezing a bit, though the sun thaws a little more each day. By next week it ought to be all gone – and will I be glad to see it go? I don't think we've ever had such a miserable winter term. The school has had radiators bursting, the woods[168] frozen up (we have to use the 'Virgin's Bower'[169], or the maids' lavs.!)

---

[167] 'Catching a crab' is the rowing term for when an oar blade is not removed from the water at the finish of a stroke, usually due to an unbalanced boat, and the oar blade therefore acts as a brake and slows the boat. A severe crab can knock the rower flat or even eject him from the boat.

[168] The 'Woods' were the outdoor toilet facilities.

[169] Virgin's Bower is a vigorous growing, deciduous, climbing Clematis plant.

I shouldn't come to the play if it is as cold as this; if you are coming, send me details of what night, how many seats etc. The first night is a fortnight Thursday, and we are having performances on Friday evening and Saturday evening. It ought to be quite good – about seven deaths I think! Unfortunately, I die off-stage!! It is a very violent play; an actor playing the part of Macbeth was fatally injured in Lancashire a month ago.[170]

Thank you very much for the money – I have spent a little of it in buying 'The Water Music' arranged for piano by Sir Granville Bantock. I am trying to learn several of the movements.

Goodbye till next week and love from Michael

The bumping race Michael referred to in his letter that caused the postponement of his school rowing race was the 1947 University Torpids.

New College rowing hard to finish head of the river in the Torpids at Oxford on Saturday. *Oxford Mail*, Monday 3rd March 1947.

---

[170] This story is true, for in 1947 the actor Harold Norman played Macbeth at the Coliseum Theatre in Oldham and in the final scene, instead of acting death on stage as rehearsed, he crawled into the wings to whisper to the stage director 'I've been stabbed'. He was taken to a hospital but died a month later as a result of the wound.

Sunday, 9th March 1947

Dear Mummy and Daddy,

Thank you ever so much for the Newsletters – it is really good to see news of the old home-town! I hope you'll go on sending them, as they are most welcome.

Last week the ice and snow had almost gone from Oxford, but on Thursday, we had our largest fall of the winter, and for one day, Oxford was practically cut off from the outside world. I believe several nearby villages are cut off. Certainly we are all down to half-rations of milk this week-end, as the farmers can't get milk into Oxford.

Yesterday we went rowing, in practice for our big race, which is next Saturday against the Pioneer boat club, composed of Old Boys of the school, I hope to be elected to the club soon – it must be one of the most exclusive rowing clubs in the country. After the race we are all going to the theatre to see the Carl Rosa Opera Company[171] perform 'Faust', and then a meal at a snack bar.

I haven't had one cigarette this term yet! I started my 'fast' as soon as I got back, and haven't had a fag since; if I did, it would spoil my wind for rowing, so I'm most definitely 'off' tobacco!

I was awarded my rowing colours on Wednesday, and I'm now wearing the colours tie and long-peaked cap.

Yesterday, while out rowing, we saw a race between Oxford College servants and Cambridge College servants. It was so funny – first the Cambridge people got the lead, then Oxford caught up and beat them!

The other day, all those who hadn't got J.T.C. boots were given coupons by the J.T.C. and told to buy a pair of clod-hoppers. I got mine; they cost 28/1d, and aren't bad, considering they weren't any coupons. I got size 10, so they ought to last!

---

[171] The Carl Rosa Opera Company had been presenting opera in English to audiences, at affordable prices, since 1893. Although it went broke in 1960, the company was revived in 1997, presenting mostly lighter operatic works.

I really can't think of any more news, so goodbye till next week and love from Michael

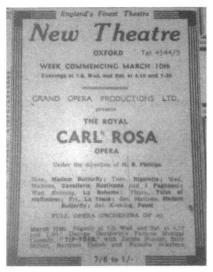

THE ROYAL CARL ROSA OPERA. *Oxford Mail*, Friday 28th February 1947

Mr. R. Weisweiller, of New College, ski-ing in central Oxford. The cyclist is Mr. J. Baker, of Wadham. *Oxford Mail*, Monday 10th March 1947

HOUSES, TREES BURIED IN COTSWOLDS. Oxford's Milk Supplies Running Short.
Oxford Mail, Thursday 6th March 1947

OXFORD WEEK-END MILK CUT A THIRD. *Oxford Mail*, Friday 7th March 1947

**NEW SNOW – BUT NEW HOPE: COAL TRAIN MOVEMENTS:
OXFORD MILK PROSPECT BRIGHTER.**
Oxford Mail, Saturday 8th March 1947

Sunday [16th March 1947]

Dear Mummy and Daddy,

What a time we're having! The floods are up again and have beaten all records – Oxford is practically surrounded by floods and the suburb of Wolvercote is flooded out, with boats going in and out of the houses. The London road is cut and the railway is covered in places. Two of the big poplars on Magdalen road[172] have been uprooted by the great gale; one of them fell across the bridge, knocking down about ten to fifteen yards of the parapet, and absolutely squashing an ice-cream van which was underneath. I believe the driver was killed.[173] The other tree is hanging right over the bridge and threatens to fall any minute; honestly, I've never seen such a gale – it blew one boy clean over while he was down in the woods!

On Saturday night we had our rowing dinner at the George and then went to the theatre to see Emlyn William's play 'Dear Evelyn', which was very good. The Old Boys who had arranged the outing paid, despite our protests, and as there were 15 or 16 of us, with dinner at

---

[172] Michael is probably referring to the Magdalen Bridge part of the High Street, rather than Magdalen Road.
[173] Thankfully, Michael was wrong about the driver's death. The occupants of the ice-cream van both survived, see newspaper report in the *Oxford Mail*, Monday 17th March 1947.

6/- a head and seats at the theatre 5/6, plus several glasses of beer apiece, it must have cost them a pretty penny.

One of them I can remember a prefect when I first came here; he must have been about 18 then – now he is about 25 and married!

A friend of mine who was in this study a year ago, but has since left, is in the army in Palestine; he's stationed at Haifa, probably the liveliest place out there, and he tells us in his letters how he has to take a loaded rifle to the pictures or wherever he wants to go; also he tells us some of the films the troops see in the Army film shows – mostly Mary Pickford and Charley Chaplain's earliest silents!

The play starts on Thursday, and we are in the thick of it with rehearsals etc., the dress rehearsal is on Tuesday.

Thank you ever so much for the parcel – that sandwich cake was fine, so was the mince-pie. Remember the 'Newsletter' this week!

On Friday, 23 of us took our final J.T.C. exam – Cert.'A' Part 2, and we all passed; I did pretty well with 79%; if I hadn't messed up my Bren Machine gun I'd have done much better. The officer asked me what regiment I'd like to join and I said the Cheshire's; he seemed quite pleased and said that you can state your preference for regiments nowadays. I really must stop now, so till next week all the best, from Michael.

DEAR EVELYN. The *Oxford Times*, Friday 7th March 1947.

During mid-March 1947, warmer air hit the UK and thawed the snow lying on the ground. This snowmelt ran off the frozen ground straight into rivers, in addition it was the wettest March in the UK for over 300 years. As a result widespread flooding occurred across Britain. More than 100,000 properties were affected and the Army and foreign aid agencies were forced to provide humanitarian aid. It is recorded as the worst overall 20th century flood of the River Thames, affecting much of the Thames Valley.

A. Jefferies, Oxford City goalkeeper, paddling along the Abingdon Road, Oxford.
Oxford Mail, Monday 17th March 1947

A bus making its way through rising floods at Marston, Oxford.
Oxford Mail, Monday 17th March 1947

Some of the damage done to Magdalen Bridge, Oxford, by fallen poplars.
Oxford Mail, Monday 17th March 1947

On Sunday 16th March 1947 winds over the UK reached 55-100 mph, causing many trees to be blown down.

The wreckage of a van on which a tree fell near Rose Lane, Oxford, last night.
Oxford Mail, Monday 17th March 1947

TWO NARROW ESCAPES FROM DEATH. Oxford Dramas of Crashing Trees.
Oxford Mail, Monday 17th March 1947

Michael's friend who was now serving with the Army in Haifa, Palestine, certainly was in a lively place. Britain governed Palestine under a League of Nations mandate from 1920 to 1948, but had become the enemy of both the peoples it was attempting to keep peace between, the Jews and the Palestinian Arabs. With neither group achieving what it was asking and fighting for, and the British unable to influence developments, the British looked for a way out.

In 1947, the newly formed United Nations accepted the idea to partition Palestine into a zone for the Jews (Israel) and a zone for the Arabs (Palestine). With this United Nations proposal, the British withdrew from the region on May 14th 1948. Between September 1945 and December 1948, 914 British servicemen lost their lives in the conflict.

PIPELINE BOMB START HAIFA'S BIGGEST FIRE. *Oxford Mail*, Monday 31st March 1947

BRITISH SOLDIER SHOT DEAD. GUNMEN'S RAID NEAR HAIFA.
Oxford Mail, Wednesday 2nd April 1947

Summer (Trinity) Term 1947

After almost seven years of boarding at the MCS School House on The Plain, Michael embarked on his twenty-first and final term in Oxford. The view from the School House, which had become so familiar to Michael and the other boarders, was to change forever, as the remaining part of the old St Clement's Church graveyard and the Boer War memorial were soon to be removed from the 'roundabout'.

The remaining part of the old St. Clement's churchyard, Oxford, and the Boer War memorial, at the Plain, scheduled for removal as soon as possible. *Oxford Mail*, Thursday 1st May 1947

Sunday 4th May 1947

Dear Mummy and Daddy,

Well, my last May Day is over and done with; I expect you would like to hear what I did.

As it was raining like mad in the morning after 9 o'clock, I was unable to go cycling, but I got up at 5.45 to go up the Tower, and I sang in the choir as a alto! I was rather glad that I could sing on the Tower for the last time, but was it cold??!!

I came down and watched the Morris Dancers down by the school for a bit; then after breakfast I went into town and spent the morning in gramophone shops playing records; in the end I bought Mozart's Horn Concerto, which is a fine thing. After lunch Andrew and I went to the pictures to see 'Temptation Harbour' – quite a good British film. Then in the evening I went with several people to the Theatre to see an extremely funny play called 'Off the Record' by Stephen King-Hall and Ian Hay[174]. I don't think I've laughed so much at a play – it really was a wonderful comedy, mainly about an M.P. and a naval officer who change places – the adventures of the M.P. when he tries to command a ship were especially funny.

Yesterday was very sunny and very hot here. I took a junior cross country run (for about 3 miles!) and then went to have my sunglasses repaired which job was done in five minutes, free of charge! I just produced that card and the rest was easy.

Next Sunday I am going to a big concert of Handel's Coronation anthems (or did I tell you that last week?) (!)

The Hallé Orchestra are coming here later on this month and do you think I can have the money put on the bill? I won't be going to the flicks much this term, and concerts are good educational value?

I'm making a steady income out of my stamp collection, which is selling quite well; I've just sold several shillings' worth of Dinky Toys, but no books! I am going to sell that cricket bat to the cricket club – they ought to give me 10/- or so for it.[175]

That's all for now so all the best from Michael

---

[174] Ian Hay was the pen name of Major General John Hay Beith, CBE (1876 – 1952), a British schoolmaster and soldier, who is best remembered as a novelist, playwright, essayist and historian.

[175] In 1947, 10/- (10 shillings) would have the same spending worth of approximately £18 in 2018 terms.

P.S. I've got my stripe at last! – I am now a Lance-Corporal in the J.T.C!!?!!

BIGGER CROWDS AT OXFORD MAY DAY CEREMONY. 'In view of double summer time[176], the ceremony took place at 7 a.m. instead of the usual 6 a.m. and this was one reason perhaps why the crowd was the largest for two or three years.'
Oxford Mail, Thursday 1ˢᵗ May 1947

Morris dances in Cowley Place. [the 1928 'temporary' buildings of MCS are seen in the background]
Oxford Mail, Thursday 1ˢᵗ May 1947

---

[176] Wartime BDST (British Double Summer Time) when clocks were two hours ahead of GMT during the summer months had ended in 1945. However, in 1947, due to the severe fuel shortages, clocks were advanced by one hour on two occasions during the spring and put back by one hour on two occasions during the autumn, meaning that Britain was back on BDST during the summer of 1947.

TEMPTATION HARBOUR. *Oxford Mail,* Friday 2nd May 1947

OFF THE RECORD. *Oxford Mail,* Friday 2nd May 1947

HANDEL CORONATION ANTHEMS. *The Oxford Times,* Friday 2nd May 1947

HALLÉ ORCHESTRA. *The Oxford Times,* Friday 2nd May 1947

Sunday 25th May 1947

Dear Mummy and Daddy,

It's 'eights week' at Oxford now, and since Thursday the bumping races have been in full swing; I have been to watch the first division races both nights so far. On Thursday night, Magdalen bumped into second place, and since then have been making vain efforts to catch Trinity, who are Head of River; on Friday they nearly did it, but last night, Trinity were a couple of lengths clear.

On Thursday we are shooting at Kingsbury, near Coventry, at the Midland Public Schools meeting. I'm not shooting in the team, but might be a reserve. Already this term I have shot in the team against the University and again against All Hallows School. We are shortly having matches against Winchester and Eton; I hope I can shoot in these.

The hotels are unable to put you up for Commem. Friday, so I'll have to try some of the 'bed-and-breakfast' places, of which there are several good establishments. I'm going to see about it in a few minutes!

It's a beautiful day here today, although we had a nasty storm here yesterday morning. I'm going out on the field to work soon.

If there's something good on at the New Theatre or the Playhouse on Commem. or during the following week I'll book seats. I'm sure you'd like the New Theatre, it's easily the best I've ever been in, and they have all the best plays here.

I went to see the closing overs of the South African innings at the Parks, and saw one of the Africans get a century; he was hitting out like mad.[177]

---

[177] The South African 'hitting out like mad' was Ken Viljoen, who remained undefeated on 110 at the end of the day, with the match drawn. Interestingly the captain of Oxford was Martin 'Squib' Donnelly, a New Zealand Test cricketer between 1937-49, who earlier that year (8th February 1947) had represented England at Rugby Union versus Ireland at Lansdowne Road. Both Donnelly and Alan Melville, the South African captain, won Wisden Cricketer of the Year in 1948.

By the way, I've put my name down to go on a week's training with a tank regiment early in August. It will be very good experience for me, I think, as it will be under normal Army conditions; (we won't be under canvas, but in huts). The course won't cost much, if anything, and I hope you don't mind me going.

Could you please send my old tweed jacket as soon as possible please?

Love from Michael

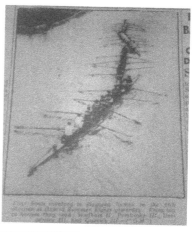

Top left: Close racing in the Oxford Summer Eights, which began this afternoon.
Top right: Four boats involved in disputed bumps in the fifth division at Oxford Summer Eights yesterday.
Bottom left: The animated scene outside the O.U. Boat House after a race at the Summer Eights as the crews bring in their boats.
Bottom right: The Trinity crew throwing each other into the Isis after winning the headship of the river at the conclusion of the Summer Eights at Oxford last night.
Oxford Mail, 22nd - 26th May 1947

Left: The rival captains – A. Melville (South Africa) and M.P. Donnelly
(Oxford University) – inspecting the cricket pitch to-day at Oxford.
Top right: **S. AFRICANS SCORE WELL AT OXFORD**. A fine partnership between
Mitchell and Melville was a feature of the South Africans innings in the Parks at
Oxford to-day. They added 125 in 85 minutes.
Bottom right: K.G. Viljoen, one of the two South African batsmen to score centuries
in the Parks at Oxford yesterday.
Oxford Mail, 21st – 23rd May 1947

Sunday 15th June 1947

Dear Mummy and Daddy,

As you can guess, I'm getting excited about Commem., and I expect it
will be the best yet for us all.

I expect you're eager to hear what I did last Monday; really, it was a
wonderful day. I got up at 7a.m. and got the 8.20 'through' train to
Beaconsfield, arriving at Grove House at about 10.15 (I had my bike in

the guard's van). After coffee and chocolate cream cake, Uncle Shirley suggested a day in London, which shook me somewhat! Anyway, by 11 o'clock we were on our way. Arriving at Marylebone, I left my bike at the left luggage place and we went to lunch at the Mayfair[May Fair] Hotel![178] In great state we drank sherry before the meal in the lounge, then went in for food. First, the most marvellous hors d'oeuvre I've ever had (mussels etc) then 'minute-steak' done to a turn, with onions all frizzled-up and special chips. After that, the sweet; about four different varieties of blancmange and jelly with clotted-up cream. I drank lager with my lunch, followed by coffee and port. After that we went to the pictures (11/6 seats at the 'Empire' Leicester-Square, Europe's biggest cinema). The film we saw was 'The Yearling', the best American film I've ever seen – it was most beautifully photographed in colour. Make sure of seeing it when it comes to Stafford.

After the film, Uncle Shirley and I went by tube to Marylebone, where we said goodbye and he gave me a £1 note. Then I cycled across to Paddington Station and caught a train home. It was a wonderful day. So as to remember it, I spent 10/- of the note in buying the records of Elgar's 'Cockaigne' Overture, which is a grand work inspired by London.

Magdalen College have lent us an 'VIII' so we now have a boat for the Royal Oxford Regatta on August bank Holiday. It would be fine if the Fletchers could motor you down for the day. I will be rowing '4', that is, the 4th one from the front, and in many ways the 2nd most important after 'stroke'.

Anyway, I'm looking forward to seeing you on Friday, so goodbye for now from

Michael.

---

[178] During the war the May Fair Hotel continued to be the place for high society to meet and party. Moving its ballroom to a lower level it entertained thousands of guests eager to dance and momentarily escape the thoughts of war. In 1942 it had suffered bomb damage that closed its first and seventh floors. This didn't prevent it being used to billet thirty US officers in 1943.

Sunday July 6th 1947

Dear Mummy and Daddy,

I've quite a lot to tell you this week about what I did yesterday, as I went to see Henley Regatta on the pillion of another boy's motorbike. We left School at 1-45, and got to Henley in time for the 2.45 race, which was the Princess Elizabeth Cup.[179] Shrewsbury were racing Bedford, and Bedford won. Then we gradually squeezed our way through the crowd until we had a perfect vantage point, right on the bank, where we could see almost the whole course. By this time the big race for the Grand Challenge Cup, was about to begin and a Cambridge crew, from Jesus College, beat a Dutch crew, the 'Delftsche Sport', by 1¼ lengths. The course is 1¼ miles long, and we were just by the mile post; the two crews were <u>dead level</u> till 300 yards from the end, when Jesus College put on a tremendous spurt, actually <u>45-46</u> strokes per minute! They got home 1 ¼ lengths ahead of the Dutch crew in a most amazing race.

Then came the second most important race, the 'Diamond Sculls', in which Kelly,[180] a huge American with a tiny little green hat on the top of his head beat the Norwegian, Frondsal [Fronsdal (initials C.H.)], by a terrific distance. We also saw two American crews racing – Kent School U.S.A. beat Tabor Academy by 1 length.[181]

---

[179] The Princess Elizabeth Challenge Cup is the most prestigious schoolboy 1st VIII rowing race of the year, inaugurated in 1946, to mark, the then Princess, Elizabeth's first visit to the Henley Regatta.

[180] John Brendan 'Jack' Kelly, Jr. (1927 – 1985), was eventually a four-time Olympian and an Olympic bronze medal winner. In 1947, Kelly was awarded the James E. Sullivan Award as the top amateur athlete in the United States and in 1948 he competed for the US in the London Olympics.

[181] Tabor Academy, understanding the British school crews did not have sufficient food during the post war years when rationing was still in force, thought the honourable undertaking was to train for the Thames Challenge Cup event under the same calorific restrictions as the British crews. Although Tabor reached the final, they lost to their traditional rival Kent School, who brought along their own provisions from the U.S., but Tabor won much support from the British fans and press for their sportsmanship.

Jamison and Gleave of Magdalen College, lost to two London Rowing club men in the final of the 'Silver Goblets', which is rowed in two-oared boats.[182] After the last race I saw Mr. Blackwell[183] to speak to for a minute. Then we went to into the huge funfair on the river bank, and watched all the buggy folks enjoying themselves as much as anyone on the dodge'ms and the 'Wall of Death'. It was a wonderful gathering – all old rowing men were there in their beautiful pink London Boat Club caps. One of them looked just like this

A real old Chinstrap[184]!

Another one, (who must have rowed in about the 1870 boat race) looked like this:

I would guess his age at least 80!

---

[182] The full title for the cup is the Silver Goblets & Nickalls' Challenge Cup. The Magdalen men racing were J.R.W. Gleave and D.G. Jamison.

[183] Basil Blackwell had previously won an event at Henley Regatta when racing for Merton College in the 1920 Visitors' Cup (for Coxless Fours). Three of the Merton crew were actually Old Mertonians, including Blackwell who had obtained his degree from Merton in 1911.

[184] One of the main characters in the BBC radio comedy programme 'It's That Man Again', was called Colonel Chinstrap, who was always full of bluster and drink.

At last we started home. One route stopped at three pubs, one of which sold Bass's best XXX bitter from the barrel. I had supper at Avery's house (the boy whose motor-bike it was) and we had fried eggs and chips, strawberries + cream; chocolate ices, and beer. Then he fetched me down to school, and so, at 10p.m., ended a wonderful day, which made up for not going to Bisley easily.[185]

Higher Cert starts a week tomorrow, and I'm busy swotting. The School Cert. people (including Andrew and Bill) have been at it for a week now; their exam finishes a week Wednesday.

I'm glad you enjoyed yourselves on your holiday and at the Ryton festivities, I would have loved to have been there.

That's all for now, so until next week, love from Michael

P.S. You owe old Hine 2 coupons – his address is 52, High Street, Oxford[186]

THURSDAY, 3 JULY, 1947

A general view at the opening day of Henley Regatta yesterday, showing the Kent School, USA (left) winning their heat in the Thames Challenge Cup event from Maidenhead. *Oxford Mail*, Thursday 3rd July 1947

---

[185] A mild outbreak of German measles prevented the school shooting team from travelling to compete at Bisley.

[186] 'Old Hine' was William P. Hine of *Hine & Son Tailors*. The Tailor shop occupied 52 High Street from 1902 until it moved to Wantage in 1998. The building is now occupied Mr Simms Olde Sweet Shoppe.

Interestingly, Michael included a helicopter, a relatively new development, in the background of his 'Diamond Sculls' sketch at the end of his 6th July 1947 letter.[187] Whether or not one had flown over the regatta during Michael's visit to Henley is not known, but helicopters were coming more to the public's attention and were starting to be seen in the skies. Indeed, exciting and newsworthy, a helicopter of a similar profile to Michael's sketch had recently featured on two occasions in the *Oxford Mail*. Little did he know at the time, but Michael would eventually end up flying helicopters as a career in the army.

---

[187] The silhouette of the helicopter indicates that it was possibly a Westland WS-51 Dragonfly, which was produced for both military and civilian use. Helicopters, still very much at an early stage in their design and development, had not featured significantly in the war, with the Sikorsky R-4/Hoverfly the only Allied helicopter to serve, when it was used primarily for rescue, in areas with harsh terrain, such as Burma and Alaska. The helicopter's appearance at Henley would have been an exciting sight.

The first commercial helicopter (a U.S. Sikorsky S.51) to land and take off in London.
Oxford Mail, Thursday 12th June 1947

The helicopter which brought Mr G.S. Lindgren, M.P. Parliamentary Secretary to the Ministry of Civil Aviation, from his home at Welwyn Garden City ….
Oxford Mail, Monday 23rd June 1947

Sunday 13th July 1947

Dear Mummy and Daddy,

I'm writing this just before bed – sorry not before, as I was asked out to Potter's for the day. (I slept the sleep of the slightly inebriated for two hours this afternoon!)

My higher Cert. begins tomorrow with a 2½ hour paper on European History, which is the worst, and the one I'm most likely to do badly in – then the rest of the exams come one a day for nine days – and on the 22nd I am a free man. On Friday, I had my last school lessons, and felt no pangs of regret either!!!

I am representing the school in the sculls at Egham Regatta on Saturday, so it's early nights and plenty of food this week. The other night I recorded the best time for the course for several years in a whiff[188] – five

---

[188] A whiff was a narrow sculling boat, fitted with outriggers, and usually of clinker build, but light and handy. It replaced the older wager boat, but has itself been superseded by the Best Boat and Modern Shell.

furlongs and a half in 4 mins. 35 secs. My previous best, done two nights previously was 4m[ins]. 47[secs], so I'm getting much better, and everyone thinks, that as long as I get a boat which suits me, I ought to do well in my races.

This evening Dobereiner and myself, both beginners at tennis, gave everyone a shock by almost beating the school second pair, Lyndon + Smith. They won the first set (6-0), then we won the second 6-2, as they weren't playing properly. The last set came, and although they started to play properly, we won four games to their six. A very good match, enjoyed by all.

G.D. Clapperton is coaching the first IV for its races at the regatta on Saturday, and my goodness, does he swear![189]

I wrote to the other Clappertons and had a lovely reply inviting me out to tea. They have moved to Wolvercote now, and, I'm going next week.

My bike is being repaired – a puncture and broken brakes, and as I'm not very wealthy ….. please ….. about 3/6? …. Thank you!

All love, (hoping to pass Highers) . . . Michael.

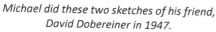

Michael did these two sketches of his friend,
David Dobereiner in 1947.

---

[189] George Douglas 'Jock' Clapperton had coxed the Oxford University boat in the 1923 and 1924 Boat Races, winning in 1923. He went on to umpire the 1959, 1961 and 1967 Boat Race. His brother R.H. Clapperton (MCS 1905-12) also coxed the Oxford boat in 1913, and then stroked the Oxford 2nd boat in 1914.

Postscript

Michael Hickey, Self-portrait, October 29th 1946.

The glorious weather in Michael's final term of school brought down a curtain of tranquillity and beauty on his school days that he was to cherish for the rest of his life. His final few weeks in his beloved school went by 'without knowing' and only when he sang the customary end-of-term hymn 'God be with you till we meet again', did he realise that it was all over and 'hot tears briefly flowed'. Michael described that he had finally 'been pushed off the ramp and was in free flight'. Back home in Stafford, as he awaited 'with a curious lack of expectation' for his results,[190] now turned eighteen, his National Service call up papers arrived, directing him to report to an address in Stoke-on-Trent. Michael duly utilised the bus warrant and the two-shilling postal order, issued with his call up papers to enable travel to the Potteries and to buy sustenance on the way, and arrived at a grim board school building along with about fifty other youths for a 'less than perfunctory'

---

[190] Michael achieved his Higher Certificate of the Oxford and Cambridge Schools Examination Board having satisfied the examiners in English and History and the subsidiary subject of Drawing.

medical examination. When asked for a specimen of urine most of the young men, including Michael, dehydrated and not able to go, were at a loss what to do, until one of the group, who had spent his postal order in a nearby pub, offered to share his full bladder. The resulting samples satisfied the medical orderly and the group were all adjudged fit for military service. A story that Michael loved to recount was that of his subsequent interview with the recruiting officer, in a cigarette-smoke filled room. When asked for his first choice of regiment, he dutifully replied 'Cheshires', as that had been his father's regiment during the Great War. Then, unexpectedly asked for a second choice and not wanting to be seen unknowledgeable, as he had not a clue, he panicked, spotted the skulls and crossbones on the officer's uniform and croaked 'Death's Head Lancers, Sir'. The officer, until this point apathetic and muffled, blazed with fury 'No such bloody regiment. Can't you see, you clown, that I am an officer of the 17th/21st Lancers?' After a feeble apology 'Er, no, sorry Sir', Michael was sent on his way with one last bark from the Lancer, 'Your ignorance won't take you far and God help the Cheshires if they're unlucky enough to get a weed like you. Now bugger off'.

Four months after leaving school, on 5th November 1947, Michael reported to a transit camp just outside Liverpool at the unfortunate address of Poverty Lane, Maghull. Confronted with a collection of drab accommodation huts, occupied by demobilising Polish soldiers, Michael decided to make straight for the NAAFI canteen. There, to his joy, he found a fellow MCS pupil, Michael Pratelli, who had joined MCS on the same day as Michael in 1939. They were to remain great friends.

Michael and the other National Service recruits congregated at Maghull were shipped over to Belfast, Northern Ireland, and found themselves in the 28th Training Battalion. The 28th TB was principally for those who had done Higher Certificates and School Certificates and Cert. A Part I and II of the Cadet Corp, and thus had good potential to become NCOs and officers. Michael described the training he received as 'very severe' and like being 'put through the mill, but it was the best thing that ever happened to me …. within six weeks I reckon I knew where I wanted to spend the rest of my life'. He had toyed with the idea of being an art student and had arrived at Palace Barracks with long hair, corduroy trousers and a floppy tie. He was soon disabused of that, given a pudding basin haircut and within two months he'd put on about two stone in weight, mostly bone and muscle and, instead of being a weed, was getting supremely fit as an infantryman.

Selected for officer cadet training with the cadet company of 28th Training Battalion at Grey Point, Helen's Bay, he was hammered into shape in preparation for going on to Officer Cadet School. After successfully passing to go to Eton Hall Officer Cadet School, Chester, in May 1948, he decided to go one step further and apply to the regular commissions board for a cadetship at Sandhurst. Thus, only one year after leaving school, in August 1948 he found himself at Sandhurst. He described Sandhurst as having 'all the brutalising attributes of a late nineteenth century, third rate, public school' but endured his sixteen months there to reminisce 'on the whole I rather liked it'. Michael admitted he didn't particularly distinguish himself at Sandhurst, rising to the rank of Cadet Corporal in his final term and passing out 264th in an order of merit of about 325.

After receiving his commission in December 1949, Michael served in Korea until 1952. He then retrained as a light aircraft pilot in 1952-53 and subsequently served in Malaya in operations during the emergency there in 1953 to 1955. In 1955 he was again deployed to serve in Korea, this time as a light aircraft commander, finally returning to England in 1956. Once at home, he again retrained, this time as a helicopter pilot, going on to join an experimental unit. After serving in Suez in 1956 he spent the next two years as an experimental helicopter pilot. In 1957 Michael received the sad news that his godfather 'Uncle Shirley', Shirley Timmis, the person whom he had been named after and who had helped finance his education, had died aged 82.

In 1959, Michael was to meet the girl who only months later he would marry and be with for the rest of his life. Of all the places to meet and the methods of attracting the attention of an attractive girl, waiting for emergency dental treatment (Garsington, Oxford) and complaining of the pain was the unlikely scene for Michael's first encounter with Bridget, a pretty twenty-year-old off duty nurse. At the time Bridget was half-way through her four years of State Registered Nurse training at St Bartholomew's Hospital in London. An Oxford girl, born in Iffley not far from where Michael had spent his MCS schooldays, Bridget had previously completed two years initial Nurse training at the Wingfield Orthopaedic Hospital (now the Nuffield), Oxford. Michael was smitten with the young nurse and a whirlwind romance blossomed. The following summer, on Saturday 9th July 1960, the two were married at St. Peter-in-the-East Church in Oxford. Michael's choirmaster and the Magdalen College organist for his first two years at MCS, William Mckie, who had been very kind to Michael in his first fledgling term as a chorister, promised Michael that if he ever got married he would play the organ for him at his wedding. Twenty years after the promise, Mckie, who by this stage had been Knighted for his services to the Queen after directing the music for her wedding in 1947 and her subsequent Coronation in 1953, was good to his word and played the organ at Michael and Bridget's wedding service, accompanied by the Magdalen Choir. In the lead-up to the wedding Mckie invited Michael and Bridget to supper at Westminster so that they could choose the music. After supper at his home in Little Cloister they were taken to the organ loft in the darkened Abbey where Mckie played their list of requests, a personal organ recital in an empty Abbey 'so as to steady your nerves' Mckie quipped.

In 1961 Michael went to the Staff College at Camberley, then served from 1962 to 1963 in East Africa flying helicopters in Kenya, Tanzania, Uganda and Zanzibar in counter-guerrilla operations. He then served in the Staff Headquarters Middle East in Aden for two years before moving to join the 4th Guards Brigade for two years at Iserloh, Westphalia in Germany, commanding a helicopter unit. It was while Michael was serving in Aden that he received the sad news that his father had died, aged 66.

After attending the Joint Services Staff College, in Chesham in 1967, Michael served as military assistant to the Chief of Staff in Headquarters Far East in Singapore. After twelve months in Singapore he was promoted and took command of the Army Air Corps in West Malaysia until the evacuation of British forces a year later. Returning to Germany he then commanded a helicopter regiment based at Detmold, Westphalia, which was the first British unit to be equipped with SS-11 anti-tank missiles. Michael was sent to be an instructor for two 'very happy' years in the early 1970s at the Royal Military College of Science at Shrivenham. Michael took a sabbatical period in 1974 to study as a Defence Fellow at the University of London, Kings College, researching the history and development of the British Army's battlefield aerial vehicles. After a brief return to Germany in 1975-6, at the headquarters of the British Army of the Rhine, Michael came back to the UK to command the Joint Air Transport Establishment (JATE) at the Royal Air Force base, Brize Norton. He always revelled working with and gaining experiences of the other services and in 1976 he made his first parachute descent at the age of 47. Always believing that 'anybody who voluntarily left a serviceable aircraft in mid-air was in need of urgent psychiatric attention', Michael put himself through the jump ordeal because he was serving with elite soldiers whom he was having to order to carry out dangerous parachuting operations, and wanted to understand how frightening the job was. After two jumps and being unceremoniously picked from his landing spot, the English Channel, in his wet-suit, he was filled full of champagne by his loyal soldiers and returned to his desk.

After commanding the JATE Michael spent two and a half years in the Operational Requirements department of the MOD and visiting the major aviation and aerospace companies across the world formulating the requirements for future army helicopters. This role saw him do the last flying of his army career, as he piloted and tested the latest helicopters from the major armed countries of the United Nations. In 1981, after thirty-four years in the Army and a rise to the rank of Colonel, General Staff Ministry of Defence, he was invited to retire from the army and take up a role of secretary to a defence lobby group 'Defence Begins at Home'. This he did until 1986 when he then became self-employed doing freelance consultancy work within the aviation and charity sectors and spending time writing. In September of the same year Michael's mother, Eveline, sadly died aged 85.

During his self-employment and retirement Michael wrote a number of books, including *Out of the Sky, A History of Airborne Warfare* (1979), *The Unforgettable Army: Slim's XIVth Army in Burma (50 Years on)* (1992); *Gallipoli: A Study in Failure* (1998); *The Korean War: The West Confronts Communism 1950-1953* (1999); *The First World War, Vol. 4: The Mediterranean Front 1914-1923 (Essential Histories)* (2002); *Single-Handed: A Wartime Romance* (2008); *The First World War: The War to End All Wars* (2013), and contributed to numerous publications including *Battle, The Army Quarterly and Defence Journal, British Army Review*, and the *RUSI (Royal United Services Institute) Journal*. In 2000 he was awarded the Westminster medal for Military Literature. He was also a guest lecturer on Holt's Battlefield Tours where he was able to share his knowledge of the Gallipoli campaign bringing alive the personal stories of those who served.

Michael and Bridget had two boys, Miles in 1962 and James in 1972, and after constant relocation involved with army life the family eventually settled to live happy and active lives, first in Winchester from 1978 and then in retirement from 2005 in rural Berkshire, Kintbury. For Michael, music was his greatest passion, and throughout his life he kept in touch with his chorister roots, singing in several choirs during various postings with the Army, local choirs in Winchester and Kintbury and becoming a member of the Waynflete Singers, based at Winchester Cathedral, being its chairman for six years. Michael's links to William Waynflete, via MCS and Winchester, led him to introduce the Waynflete Obit, an annual memorial service, held in Winchester Cathedral on the anniversary of William Waynflete's death (11th August 1486). Michael never lost touch with his old school and was an active member of its alumni club, known as the Old Waynfletes (OWs). For many years he ran an Old Waynfletes lunch in Salisbury which morphed into the Veteran Old Waynfletes (VOW) lunch for those who had left MCS forty or more years ago. The VOW lunch continues to be held at MCS every year. He had a wonderful sense of fun, he rowed with the OWs, proposed toasts at OW dinners and once landed a helicopter at his old school in 1959 on his way to a military camp. He had an amazing memory and recollection of his own and his father's and grandfather's time at MCS, and as such he was a much-valued source of information to the school archive. In November 2013 Michael Hickey passed away after a brave battle with cancer. Bridget, his wife for fifty-three years, remains at the centre of the Kintbury community, constantly fielding the messages and emails that still arrive for Michael concerning his books and articles.

The characters in the letters

For reference, a brief background of each of the main characters mentioned by Michael in his letters or in the other chapters is given below:

Sir Hugh Allen, was an English musician who was a leading influence on British musical life in the first half of the 20th century. A Professor of Music at Oxford and the Director of Music at The Royal College of Music (1918-37) he is recognised as being both an academic and administrator of music. Sadly, he was to die as a result of a road accident in February 1946, at the age of seventy-six.

Vera Jane Ashby (née Hickey), **Aunty Vera**, was Michael's father's sister. Vera married William C. Ashby in 1929, but by the time the war had started was widowed and living back with her parents in Trowell, Nottingham.

John Clarke **Avery**, was a schoolboy at MCS from January 1939 until 1947. After leaving MCS he joined the army and went to the Royal Military Academy, Sandhurst, at the same time as Michael. Avery spent his whole career in the army, eventually rising to the rank of Lieutenant Colonel in the Royal Artillery.

Basil Henry **Blackwell**, was a publisher and bookseller (Blackwell's Bookshop) who was a pupil at MCS from 1901-07 before gaining a Classical Scholarship at Merton College in 1907. After obtaining his degree in 1911, Blackwell continued to represent Merton at rowing, being a member of their 1st VIII in 1912 and 1913. On leaving MCS he became an active member of the Old Boys' Club (becoming Secretary then President) and was also coached rowing at the school for more than a decade, from 1910. In 1924 he had become the head of Blackwell's family bookshop and publishing business (in Broad Street, Oxford). He later became Chairman on the School's Board of Governors and eventually a Benefactor to the School. He was knighted for services to publishing in 1956.

Eric Brereton, **'Uncle' Eric**, was a close friend and police colleague (Chief Inspector) of Michael's father in Staffordshire. Michael was friendly with his son, Geoffrey.

Geoffrey Brereton, was Michael's close friend who lived in his home town of Stafford.

Michael and his friend from Stafford, Geoff Brereton (holding spade), at Colwyn Bay in c.1937.

Others in the photo: Back: Brian Hickey and Eric Brereton; Middle: Nelly Brereton, Eveline Hickey and 'Granny' Brereton; young girl: Sheila Haggis.

Brian Fitzroy **Cairns,** was in the same academic year as Michael, and although he only joined MCS in the summer term of 1943, he and Michael very soon became best friends. Brian left MCS the year after Michael, in 1948 and, after attending Pembroke College, returned to MCS to teach English for the first two years of his teaching career. His pastime and passion of art culminated in his portrait painting of Sir Basil Blackwell, which now hangs at the entrance to the school's 'Sir Basil Blackwell Library'.

The Clappertons, friends of Michael's parents, lived at Sandford-on-Thames, four miles south of Oxford, and part owned the 'Cannon and Clapperton' Paper Mill, downstream from Oxford and adjacent to the Sandford Lock. The Clapperton brothers, R.H., J.F. and J.D. had all been at MCS with Michael's father in the early 1900s.

Graham Lesley **Coleman**, joined MCS as a boarder and chorister in 1935. Originally from Shoreham in Sussex, on leaving school at the end of 1943 he joined the forces in early 1944.

David Alfred **Cornell**, schoolboy at MCS from 1934-40 and a Senior Prefect from 1938-40.

Reverend 'Herbie' Crusha, described by Michael as 'of an alarmingly High Church persuasion' was MCS Chaplain and Scoutmaster from 1941-44. After leaving MCS Edwin W.H. Crusha went on to be the Chaplain at Ardingly College, then Vicar of Saint Saviour's, Saltley in the Diocese of Birmingham.

Mr Davis, known as **'Pa D'**, the headmaster or 'Master' of MCS from 1930 to 1944. Michael reminisced that Rushworth Kennard Davis 'appeared formidable on first acquaintance but was not only a fine classics scholar but a cultured wit who, in retirement, continually won 'Spectator' competitions with his light verse' and as well as being headmaster and classics teacher 'ran the administration of the school without recourse to secretary or typewriter'. In 1931 Davis wrote the prayer 'The Lilies of the Field', which was eventually put to music by H.C. Stewart to become the school hymn. Davis' wife, affectionately referred to by the boys as **'Ma D'**, was a stalwart of the school and would provide teas for sports fixtures, a difficult undertaking during rationing.

David Angus **Donaldson**, a fellow chorister of Michael's at MCS, albeit two years more senior. **'Dopey'** Donaldson joined MCS in September 1938 and appears to have left after his voice broke in 1941.

Mr Elam, joined MCS as the new housemaster in September 1940. A recent Maths graduate from The Queen's College, Oxford, Horace Elam was unable to join the armed forces because of a bout of near-fatal peritonitis after an appendix operation just before his final exams. Michael remembered how Elam had joined MCS in a 'pathetically weak' and 'enfeebled condition' and although recovering a degree of health he never achieved a level of health to qualify him for military service. Elam re-invigorated the school scout troop (the 40th Oxford) and in the summer holidays masterminded agricultural camps when groups of dayboys and boarders alike lived under canvas on the estate of Lord St Audries at Cricket St Thomas in Somerset helping with the harvest.

He also led the school dramatic society and produced numerous plays. Horace Elam was to remain at MCS all his life and became one of MCS's institutions, sadly dying shortly before his retirement in 1976.

Mr Greenham, joined MCS in 1940 principally as an English and History teacher, but also taught Latin and his eventual career subject, Art. Michael described Peter Greenham as his 'most influential master at Magdalen', to whom boys 'listened spellbound', for he had a gift for 'stimulating' and 'encouraging' and getting boys to research and to find and discover from books for pleasure. Bob Stanier recognised his artistic flair and allowed him to use a shed on the school site as an artist's studio. In 1951 Greenham became an Associate and then in 1960 he became a Resident Assistant of the Royal Academy. In 1964, the year he painted Queen Elizabeth II, he became Keeper of the Royal Academy. True to Stanier's prediction he became a renown portraitist.

Tutorial drawing by Peter Greenham from Michael's school sketch book

Mrs Halsey, the Matron of the school for twenty-two years from 1918 to 1940, known to the boys at the school as **'Pitts'**. Elizabeth Halsey had previously worked at the school for thirteen years, from 1884 until 1897, before gaining experience as Matron in other schools. Serene and dignified in old age, she always addressed the boys with the prefix 'Mister' and was said to have owned the 'cleverest budgie in Oxford'. She died on 7th October 1954, aged eighty-four. Her nickname is believed to have originated due to her room in School House smelling like a sweaty armpit!

Captain Haseler was a chorister at MCS at the same time as Michael's father, Brian. J.V. Haseler found notoriety by 'pulling a face' and sticking his tongue out on the 1907 Magdalen College Choir photo. To hide Haseler's face and the College's embarrassment, the photo was 'airbrushed' so that Haseler appears as a smudged figure. Haseler served with the Royal Warwickshire Regiment and was wounded and awarded a DCM during the First World War. Michael recalled Haseler visiting the family home in Stafford on many occasions when he was a child.

Brain Hickey, Michael's father, co-recipient of Michael's letters at the family home of 45 Rising Brook, Stafford (referred to as **'Gangipop'** in one of Michael's letters), went to MCS himself from 1907-14 and was a Magdalen College chorister at the same time as Ivor Novello (then David Ivor Davies). Born in 1898, Brain G.L. Hickey had fought with the Cheshire Regiment and been wounded on the Somme during the First World War, when only eighteen. After the First World War he was a Prep school master in Ascot, then, after moving to Staffordshire joined the police force in 1927, before joining the regional electric company. Michael's father (Brian G.L. Hickey), great uncle (Vivian C.F. Hickey) and grandfather (Godfrey M.V. Hickey) and had all been choristers at MCS. Brian died in 1964, aged sixty-six.

Brian, Michael and Eveline
Hickey in their garden at 45
Rising Brook, Stafford in 1938

Brain Hickey in Police uniform

Eveline Hickey (née Wright), Michael's mother and co-recipient of Michael's letters at the family home of 45 Rising Brook, Stafford. Born in Warwickshire in 1901, Eveline married Brian Hickey in Nottinghamshire in 1927, when aged twenty-six. Such was her new husband's love of MCS and his recognition of the importance of its Commemoration service that he and Eveline spent their honeymoon in Oxford to go to the service and for Brian to play in the traditional Old Boys' cricket match and to attend the Old Boys' dinner. Eveline's sister, Michael's '**Aunty Effie**' lived nearby Oxford at Boar's Hill. Eveline outlived Brian by twenty-two years, spending her latter days living nearby to Michael in Winchester, dying aged eighty-five in 1986.

Brian, Michael and Eveline Hickey on the
beach at Colwyn Bay in 1938

Eveline (back right), with her two
sisters (Amy and Effie) and father
(Frederick) in 1941

Reverend Godfrey Hickey, Michael's paternal grandfather (referred to as '**Goggy**' in one of Michael's letters) was the Rector of St Helen's Church, Trowell, Nottinghamshire, and lived in the Rectory from October 1926 until November 1942. Both Godfrey M.V. Hickey and his brother, Vivian C. F. Hickey, had also attended MCS from 1885-91 and 1885-95, respectively.

Godfrey Hickey (Michael's grandfather), with Eveline and Brian Hickey in the background, at Nottingham in 1928

Mr Insley, nicknamed 'Tête d'Oeuf' (egghead), pronounced 'Tetuf', because of his large bald dome-shaped skull, joined MCS in 1940 as a sixth form geography master and temporary housemaster. Described as an 'idiosyncratic man', he spent much time teaching boys to swim, in the Cherwell next to the first white bridge, using a homemade contraption (a rubber tyre dangling from a pole) to support the boys in the water. Despite the boys occasionally being taken to the municipal swimming baths at Cowley, Insley progressed the boys through Bronze and Silver National Lifesaving awards in the river.

Miss Jarvis, known as '**Ma Ja**', was taken on as a teacher at MCS in 1941. Ismay Jarvis is believed to have been the only female teacher at the school during this time. 'Ma Ja' remained at the school for the duration of the war, departing in 1945 upon the return of the three teachers who had been away on military service.

Reverend 'Botty' Johns, geography and maths teacher and diminutive Welsh rugby coach at MCS for 37 years (1920-57), H.S. Johns was also the Vicar of Weston-on-the-Green. If the 1st XV home match was found to be short of a neutral referee 'Botty' would take the whistle and inevitably any early infringement, no matter how small, by the opponents, occurring within the range of their goal would result in a penalty and an unearned three-point lead. The embarrassment felt by the MCS spectators outweighed any advantage, so whenever it looked as though Botty was going to referee, the boys had orders to send to School House for Bob Stanier, who would hot foot it down to the pitch and take over with more comfortable impartiality. During the war years, Botty's car, an SS Jaguar[191], was the only car ever parked in Cowley Place. The SS Jaguar, widely considered one of the most aesthetically pleasing sports cars of the 1930s with a theoretical top speed of 100mph, gained Botty much respect from his pupils.

Robert James **Lawther**, joined MCS as a schoolboy in 1936, becoming a senior chorister in 1941.

Michael A. **Lewi**, joined MCS as a schoolboy during the last year of the war, eventually leaving to take up a place at Hertford College in 1949.

Michael's sketch of Michael Lewi. c.1947

---

[191] The SS Jaguar was a British 2-seat sports car built between 1936 and 1941 by SS Cars Ltd of Coventry. The 'SS' in the model and the manufacturers name was a remnant of the company's origins as Swallow Sidecars Ltd. During the Second World War, because of the Nazi connotations of the initials "SS", the company was renamed Jaguar.

Kenneth Barry **Lyndon**, the younger of the two Lyndon bothers, **'Lyndon Mi'**, was a schoolboy at MCS during the same years as Michael, from 1939 to 1947.

Patrick Beresford **Lyndon**, the older of the two Lyndon bothers, **'Lyndon Ma'**, was one year ahead of Michael at MCS, arriving in 1938 and leaving in 1946.

Dr Mallam, the medical doctor to the school. Pat Mallam's practice was in a charming old house in Holywell Street, whose internal walls were covered in antique prints and rowing oars he had won. Pat had rowed for England in the Empire Games. When Pat went off to war, his 'venerable and benign' father assumed full responsibility for the practice.

Mr Mckie, *Informator Choristarum* (Choirmaster) at Magdalen College from 1938-41. In 1941, William N. Mckie was appointed Organist and Master of the Choristers at Westminster Abbey, but was unable to take up the post until 1946 owing to war service with the RAF. He served as a pilot officer from 1941 to 1946, periodically corresponding with Michael. In 1947, McKie arranged the music for the marriage of Princess Elizabeth and the Duke of Edinburgh, and in 1953 he arranged the music for the Coronation of Queen Elizabeth II. For his services, Mckie received a knighthood in the Coronation honours of 1953. In 1960, not only did he arrange the music for the marriage of Princess Margaret to Antony Armstrong-Jones: Mckie in keeping with a promise he had made to Michael twenty years earlier, arranged the music and played the organ for Michael's wedding at St. Peter-in-the-East Church in Oxford. Mckie died in 1984, aged eighty-three, and is buried in the West Cloister of Westminster Abbey.

David Norman **Metcalfe**, school friend of Michael, joined MCS in 1939, having auditioned successfully for a choral scholarship on the same day as Michael. In 1943, Metcalfe had become Head Chorister but after mocking the relatively new choirmaster, Philip Taylor in the summer of 1944 he was expelled from the school, making way for Michael to become Head Chorister.

Ken Morley, a close school friend of Michael's, who joined MCS in January 1941.

John Platts, joined MCS as a schoolboy during the last year of the war, eventually leaving the school in 1948 to take up a place at New College.

Michael's sketch of John Platts. c.1947

William '**Bill**' G. **Potter,** was a schoolboy at MCS from 1943 to 1949.

Mr Rathbone, a swimming Master at MCS, who played the double bass in the fledgling school orchestra. After being called up in the Autumn of 1942, C.M.F. Rathbone served with the Royal Army Ordnance Corps, eventually being promoted to Lieutenant.

Andrew Downing **Saunders**, joined MCS in 1940 as a boarder. Andrew's family lived in St Austell, Cornwall, where he had previously attended Lawn Prep School. Despite being junior to Michael by two years, the two were close friends. Michael refers to his friend as 'Saunders' in his letters home between 1943-46, then refers to him by his first name in his last year at the school 1946-47.

Captain Shepperd had been a schoolboy at MCS from 1907 to 1914, exactly the same years as Michael's father, Brian. During the Great War, C.B. Shepperd served with the Border Regiment, then later with

The Buffs. Having obtained a BSc from The Queen's College, Oxford in the 1920s he subsequently been a Science Master, firstly at Southcliffe School near Filey, Yorkshire, and then at Merchiston Castle School in Edinburgh. In 1942 he came out of retirement to teach science at MCS, filling one of the gaps made by younger teachers being called up for military service. Known affectionately by the boys as 'Bumph', Shepperd also became Captain and commanding officer of the school's Junior Training Corps in September 1943. He retired, again, in December 1945.[192]

Captain Simmonds, was the Housemaster at the school when Michael joined in 1939. Having previously been in the Army and having served during the Great War, J.C. Simmonds re-joined the army at the start of 1940, eventually being promoted to Major. Universally respected and known as **'Flick'**, because of his habit of flicking chalk at any boy not focusing on his lesson, his return as Head of Chemistry in 1945, after the war, was warmly welcomed.

John Walter Gainer **Smith**, boarder at MCS from 1936-40, school prefect from 1939-40 and the prefect in Michael's dorm in his first year at the school. Upon leaving school he joined the RAF and reached the rank of Flight Lieutenant in 1945.

Jean Spinks, Michael's godmother.

Mr Stanier, was first Usher (deputy headmaster) from 1935-44, then Master (headmaster) at MCS from 1944-67. Stanier was an influential character, who together with his wife, Maida, formed a partnership which served the school for thirty-two years. During this time, Robert S. Stanier wrote 'The History of Magdalen College School, Oxford', initially publishing the First Edition in 1940 with the Oxford-based Clarendon Press, then publishing the Second Edition in 1958 with another historic

---

[192] He is not to be confused with Major C.H.B. Shepherd MC (late Manchester regiment and Machine Gun Corps) who took over as commanding officer of the MCS OTC in 1926 and in 1927 presented the school with a trophy that is still awarded each year to the most efficient Section of the Cadet Corps.

Oxford book publisher and seller, Blackwell. An active member of the Campaign for Nuclear Disarmament in post war Britain, Stanier made a lasting impression on everyone he taught. A patient, kind and liberal man, known affectionately as 'Bob', he worked tirelessly during his time to save the school from closure during the years when the College wanted to cut the financial ties with the school.

Peter Stephens, chorister at MCS from 1936. Left school in 1941 to join the Army School of Music.

Dr Stewart, returned as organist and *Informator Choristarum* to Magdalen College in 1941, after William Mckie vacated the position to join the RAF. Haldane Campbell Stewart was a great favourite with the choristers, and although growing deaf in his old age he didn't lose his amazing sense of perfect pitch. Despite his age and commitments to the College and its choir he was an active member of the Royal Observer Corps and it was said of him that he could accurately identify any type of German aircraft flying overhead from the pitch of its engines. During gaps in rehearsals in June 1942 Stewart, who had been running around playing active games with the boys despite suffering from rheumatism, fell downstairs breaking his neck and died at the age of seventy-four. He had previously been *Informator Choristarum* from 1919-38 and an old boy of MCS and the College. Stewart played first-class cricket for Kent from 1892 to 1903. In 1931 he composed the music for the prayer 'The Lilies of the Field' written by Kennard Davis, hence producing the school hymn.

Mr Taylor. Philip J. Taylor took over as Choirmaster of Magdalen College, after H.C. Stewart's sudden death in 1942. He was described by Michael as being an 'uncharismatic Informator Choristarum'.

John Stephen **Taylor**, joined MCS as a ten-year-old boarder in April 1939, from the Alpine School in Klosters, Switzerland. When Michael joined MCS the following term, the two were placed in the same Form (II) and became close friends.

Avis **Brenda Timmis** (née Hughes), **'Aunty Brenda'**. Wife of Michael's godfather, Shirley Timmis. Brenda died in 1968, aged eighty-seven.

Shirley Timmis, 'Uncle Shirley' was Michael's godfather and contributed financially to send Michael to MCS. Born in 1875, Shirley Sutton Timmis was a soap manufacturer and became The High Sheriff of Buckinghamshire in 1941. During the war Shirley and his wife, Brenda, let out their Butler's Court home as a Red Cross Hospital and lived nearby at Grove House, Beaconsfield. Shirley died in 1957.

Shirley and Brenda Timmis at Butler's Court, Beaconsfield c.1929.

Sir Henry Tizard FRS was the president of Magdalen College from 1942 to 1946, having been a student of mathematics and chemistry there just prior to the Great War. In 1933, at the age of forty-eight, Henry Thomas Tizard was appointed chairman of the Aeronautical Research Committee and had a huge input into the development of radar in the run up to the war. In 1940, backed by the British Government, he undertook the 'Tizard Mission' to the United States to convey a number of technical innovations to the U.S. in order to secure assistance with their further development while maintaining the war effort. Tizard died in 1959.

George Christopher **Turner**, from the Isle of Wight, was born just six days before Michael in 1929 and joined MCS as a chorister and boarder one term before Michael in April 1939.

Miss Wiblin, was a music and piano teacher at MCS during and for many years after the war. Christine Meredith Wiblin had a sister, Mary Wiblin, who had also been a music teacher at the school from 1927 until her sudden death in 1938. A cup for the most outstanding music contribution to the school is awarded annually in Mary Wiblin's memory.

Dr Wiggins, was an old boy of the MCS who had been at the school during the 1890s at the same time as Michael's uncle, Vivian Hickey. C.A. Wiggins, previously a Chief Medical Officer in Uganda and awarded the CMG (Companion of the Most Distinguished Order of St Michael and St George) for service overseas in connection with Commonwealth affairs, received an Honorary MA degree from Oxford in 1942 and soon afterwards was ordained Deacon to Lewknor in 1943, before becoming Vicar of Shirburn and Pyrton in 1944.

Abbreviations and Glossary

A

AFS   Auxiliary Fire Service

ARP   Air Raid Precautions. ARP wardens enforced the 'blackout', sounded air raid sirens, and guided, evacuated and rescued people caught up in air-raids.

ATS   Auxiliary Territorial Service

B

BEF   British Expeditionary Force

Brig-Gen   Brigadier General

BISF   British Iron and Steel Federation

BDST   British Double Summer Time

C

Commem.   The annual MCS commemoration service held in honour of the benefactors of the school.

Capt.   Captain

D

Dorm   Dormitory

E

Eights Week   Eights week is a four day regatta of bumps races between colleges of Oxford University. It usually takes place in May each year.

F

FANY   First Aid Nursing Yeomanry

G

GWR   Great Western Railway Company

I

Informator   Master of the choir at Magdalen College.
choristarum

J

JTC   Junior Training Corps

JATE   Joint Air Transport Establishment

L

LMS   London, Midland and Scottish Railway Company

M

mufti   plain clothes worn by a person who sometimes
                        wears uniform

MOD   Ministry of Defence

N

NFS   National Fire Service

NCO   Non-commissioned Officer

New Coll.   New College

NFS   National Fire Service

O

OCTU   Officer Cadet Training Unit

Old Waynflete   the term used for alumni of MCS, after the school's
(OW)   founder William Waynflete.   Prior to 1935 old
                        pupils from the school were simply referred to as
                        Old Boys.

OTC   Officer Training Corps

| OUDS | Oxford University Dramatic Society |
| OUOTC | Oxford University Officer Training Corps |

P

PT	Physical Training
PO	Postal Order
perm.	permission

Q

| Queen's | The Queen's (Royal West Surrey Regiment) |

R

RAF	Royal Air Force
RAMC	Royal Army Medical Corps
RFC	Royal Flying Corps

S

| The Spit | At MCS, The Spit is the small peninsular strip of land that protrudes from the south side of Magdalen Bridge, surrounded by two courses of the River Cherwell and reached by crossing the first white bridge. |

T

| Torpids | Torpids is a bumping race, a type of rowing race that takes place between college crews of Oxford University each year in the Hilary Term. |
| TTFN | Ta Ta For Now |

W

| WVS | Women's Voluntary Service |

Bibliography

The following sources were amongst those used in the research and writing of this book.

Books:

Brockliss, Laurence W.; *Magdalen College School*, Shire Publications, 2016.

Goldschmidt, Leo; Seven Nines. *A Boy's Wartime Story*, Brussels, 2005.

Graham, Malcolm; *Oxfordshire at War*. Alan Sutton Publishing Limited, 1994.

Munz, Ulrich Wolfgang, *Fire on the mind ever burning*, Nedlands, Western Australia, 2001.

Malcolmson, Patricia and Robert, *A Vicar's Wife In Oxford, 1938-1943, The Diary of Madge Martin*, Boydell and Brewer, 2018.

Stanier, Robert; *Magdalen School. A History of Magdalen College School, Oxford*, Blackwell, Oxford 1958.

Newspapers/Magazines (1939-1947):

Oxford Mail; Oxford Times (Oxfordshire History Centre)

The Lily Magazine (Magdalen College School)

Executive Intelligence Review, Volume 14, Number 22, May 29, 1987

Websites:

British History Online http://www.british-history.ac.uk/vch/oxon/vol4/pp181-259 [accessed 22 August 2018]: Eleanor Chance, Christina Colvin, Janet Cooper, C J Day, T G Hassall, Mary Jessup and Nesta Selwyn, 'Modern Oxford', in A History of the County of Oxford: Volume 4, the City of Oxford, ed. Alan Crossley and C R Elrington (London, 1979), pp. 181-259.

Audio recording:

Michael Hickey interview, 25 March 1999 (Audio recording Cat. No. 18732, Imperial War Museum, London)

Personal memoirs and correspondence:

Michael Hickey (MCS 1939-47): *MCS at War 1939-45.* Personal letters home, notes and other correspondance.

Brian T.N. Bennett (1939-45): *MCS 1939-1945.*

Peter Shier (MCS 1940-45). *MCS in the Second World War. A Memoir.*

David Trebilcock (MCS 1939-47): *Wartime memories of MCS*

J. H. McGivering (MCS 1935-41): *Some thoughts on MCS & the '39 War*

Roger M. Firkins (MCS 1941-46): *MCS memories*

David J. Mander (MCS 1942-1949): *Random thoughts*

Charles Pearson: *Memories of the Home Front in Oxford*, interview transcript, Article A7821948, Centre for Oxford Studies.

Exeter University, Centre for the Study of War, State and Society: The Bombing of Britain 1940-1945 Exhibition.

Acknowledgement for photographs:

Oxford University Images / Oxfordshire History Centre and Magdalen College School Archive, Oxford.

Every effort was made to trace the copyright owners for the images used throughout this book and I am indebted to the people and organisations mentioned in the acknowledgments above for their kind permission to reproduce their photographic images.

In the few cases where copyright owners were not traceable, if they come to light in the future the relevant acknowledgement will be published in subsequent editions of the book.

Notes

Index of People

General Index

CPSIA information can be obtained
at www.ICGtesting.com
Printed in the USA
BVHW030910100519
547951BV00001B/23/P